·303-INCH MACHINE GUNS AND SMALL ARMS.

$\dfrac{40}{\text{W.O.}}$
$\overline{2394}$

NOMENCLATURE OF PARTS, STRIPPING, ASSEMBLING, ACTION, JAMS, MISSFIRES, FAILURES, AND INSPECTION OF:

(1.) Rifles, Short, **M.L.E.**
(2.) ,,   Charger Loading **M.L.E.**
(3.) Pistols, Webley.
(4.) Gun, Maxim, ·303-inch.
(5.) Gun, Vickers, ·303-inch.

Compiled in the Field Artillery and Small Arms Branch, Ordnance College. (Revised Edition—1915.)

The Naval & Military Press Ltd

Published by

The Naval & Military Press Ltd
Unit 5 Riverside, Brambleside
Bellbrook Industrial Estate
Uckfield, East Sussex
TN22 1QQ England

Tel: +44 (0)1825 749494

www.naval-military-press.com
www.nmarchive.com

The Library & Archives Department at the Royal Armouries Museum, Leeds, specialises in the history and development of armour and weapons from earliest times to the present day. Material relating to the development of artillery and modern fortifications is held at the Royal Armouries Museum, Fort Nelson.

For further information contact:
Royal Armouries Museum, Library, Armouries Drive, Leeds, West Yorkshire LS10 1LT

Or visit the Museum's website at
www.armouries.org.uk

In reprinting in facsimile from the original, any imperfections are inevitably reproduced and the quality may fall short of modern type and cartographic standards.

MAGAZINE RIFLES IN THE SERVICE.

Long Rifles.

Magazine Lee-Metford (M.L.M.) Mark I Issued 1889.
,, ,, ,, ,, ,, I* ,, 1892.
,, ,, ,, ,, ,, II ,, 1894.
,, ,, ,, ,, ,, II* ,, 1895.
,, ,, Enfield (M.L.E.) ,, I ,, 1896.
,, ,, ,, ,, ,, I* ,, 1899.

These rifles will now be found chiefly in the R.N. and Colonial Forces. The Metford system of rifling permitted excessive wear of the barrel when cordite was used as the propellent, so the Enfield system with fewer and deeper grooves was introduced. As the Metford barrels wear out, they are replaced by Enfield barrels.

A large number of M.L.M., Mark II* and M.L.E. rifles have been converted to charger-loading; the Mark I retains the L.E. sights, Mark I* is fitted with an improved back-sight, both are known as M.L.E. charger-loading rifles and are issued to the Territorial Force. Many of the later patterns of Long Rifles have been converted to Short Rifles, known as converted Mark II, II*, and IV.

Rifle, Charger-Loading, Magazine Lee-Enfield, Mark I and I*.

Converted from M.L.M., Mark II*, and M.L.E., Mark I and I*, for the use of the Territorial Force. Mark I first issued in 1908. Mark I* first issued in 1914.

Short Rifles.

Rifle, short, Magazine Lee-Enfield, Mark I, issued 1904.
,, ,, ,, ,, ,, ,, I* ,, 1907.
,, ,, ,, ,, ,, ,, III ,, 1907.

In addition to the above, the later patterns of the Long Rifle have been converted to Short Rifles, as follows :—

R.S.M.L.E. converted Mark II, conforming to S.R. Mark I.
,, ,, ,, II* ,, ,, ,, I*.
,, ,, ,, IV ,, ,, ,, III.

The converted rifles conform to the new rifles of the same date, except for a few components taken from the old rifle and utilised in the conversion instead of manufacturing new components to the pattern adopted in Short Rifles.

The "Short Rifle" was introduced in 1904 to replace the "Long Rifle" and the "Carbine." It is issued to all branches of the Service, and the following are the chief points of difference between it and the Long Rifle:—

1. Average Marks I, I*, II and II* about 1 lb. lighter, Marks III and IV about 8 ozs. lighter.
2. Barrel smaller in diameter and 5 inches shorter.
3. Improved sighting arrangements.
4. Adapted for charger loading.
5. Trigger has a double pull-off.
6. Barrel completely covered by handguards and stock. Great attention is paid to the correct adjustment of the stock fore-end and of the nose-cap. The barrel is connected to the stock by the inner band and spring, with ·002" clearance between barrel and band. The opening in the nose-cap for the barrel is elliptical, with a spring stud to press the barrel against the top of the opening. Clearance ·002". The function of the spring stud is to retain the barrel in an unvarying position with reference to the nose-cap.
7. All rifles that have been converted and resighted for Mark VII ammunition are marked H.V. on the barrel: C.L. Rifles in front and Short Rifles behind the back-sight.

Directions for Stripping Rifles, Short, Magazine Lee-Enfield, Marks I, I* and III. Also Converted Short Rifles, Marks II, II* and IV, and C.L. Rifles.

Tools.—None but the authorised tools should be used, and then only for the purpose for which intended, *e.g.*, a small screwdriver should not be used to remove or replace large screws, nor should a large screwdriver be used for small screws, &c. The tools should be laid out on the bench to the right of the vice, close to the flower, and the component parts of the rifle, as stripped, on the left side of vice. This arrangement prevents the tools and parts of rifle from becoming mixed.

The following is a list of the tools which are supplied for use when stripping and assembling rifles:—

Designation of Tool.	No.	Use of Tool.
Anvil, stock butt, M.L.E.R.S. (Short rifles).	1	For attaching stock butts that have slightly swelled.
Anvil, stock butt, M.R., (R.C.L.).	1	
Braces, armourers	1	For use with the various bits.
Bits, screwdriver :—		
Butt plate screw	1	For removing or replacing screws butt plate.
Stock bolt	1	For removing, replacing, or tightening stock bolt.
Centre punch	1	For fixing fore-sight, also for centre-punching certain screws.
Clams, armourers, standing vice.	1	Cork or buff lined for use with the vice when gripping the rifle to prevent damage to the woodwork, &c.
Corks, clam	2	To prevent damage to fittings.
Drifts, fore-end M.L.M.R. Mark II.	1	For removal and replacement of the stock fore-end.
Drifts, pin, fixing, washer, pin axis sight back.	1	For removing and replacing the pin fixing.
Drifts, sight axis pin, M.L.M.	1	For removing axis pins.
Drifts, magazine catch-pin, M.L.M.	1	For removing catch-pins, also pins, axis, sight back, R.S.M.L.E.
Drifts, pin, fixing, stud, head catch, slide, sight, back, R.S.M.L.E.	1	For removing pins fixing.
Drifts, wire, small	1	For removing pins, stop, band lower and band outer.
Drifts, wire, large	1	For removing safety catch, M.L.E.C.L. rifles.
Drivers, Screw :— Armourers { large	1	For screws band inner, nose-cap back, guard trigger front, dial sight fixing screw and screw and nut, protector back sight. It is also used for removing the sear spring.
small	1	For screws band outer, swivels piling and butt, nose-cap front, disc marking butt, ejector, guard trigger back, sear, spring sight back, stop charger guide, and screw spring sight aperture.

(B 11155)   A 3

Designation of Tool.	No.	Use of Tool.
Drivers, screw:—		
Extractor, axis, M.L.M.	1	For screws bed back sight, cut off, extractor, keeper fine adjustment, screw nut keeper striker (early marks), and screw wind-gauge, also used for replacing the sear spring.
Fork, dial sight...	1	For screw sight dial pivot, and (with Mk. III and IV Rifles) screw catch slide back.
Implement, action, M.L.E.R. Short.	1	Various uses.
Implement, action, M.L.M.	1	Pattern "D" for M.L.E. charger loading rifles.
Horses, armourers	2	To support rifle.
Hammers, riveting, 4 oz.	1	Various uses.
Pincers, armourers	1	For removing pins or screws that stick after being unscrewed.
Pliers, flat-nose	1	Various uses.
Testers, trigger pull, Mk. II.	1	For weighing various springs.
Tools, extractor spring	1	For removing and replacing extractor spring.
Tools removing handguard No. 1	1	For removal of rear handguards of all short rifles.
No. 2	1	For removal of handguards of charger loading M.L.E. rifles.
Tools removing striker R.S.M.L.E.	1	When striker is stuck so that it cannot be removed by the bolt head.
Tools removing striker, Pattern B.	1	For use with M.L.E.C.L. rifles.
Tools removing wad stock bolt	1	For withdrawing the wad stock bolt from the butt.
Tools removing plate keeper screw wind-gauge.	1	For lifting the keeper plate from its recess.
Vices standing, 36 lb.	1	For holding the rifle while stripping.
Reflectors, mirror, S.A., ·303-inch.	1	For examining barrel.

Designation of Tool.		No.	Use of Tool.
Gauges, distance of bolt from end of chamber.	·064″	1	For testing minimum distance allowed between face of bolt-head and end of chamber.
	·074″	1	For testing maximum distance allowed between face of bolt-head and end of chamber.
Gauges, armourers. Pistol, Webley:— Hammer projection and radius of point.		1	For use with Webley pistols.
Distance of cylinder from face of body, ·052-inch rejecting.		1	
Gauges, projection of stock bolt through body.		1	To gauge and ensure that the stock bolt is properly screwed home, and that the projection is not excessive.
Gauge striker point (for height and figure).		1	Protrusion from ·04″—·042″.
Pilot pins (not a service store) coned-point, thus— ▬▬		1	Should be made as required for assisting in the replacement of axis pins for back sights, &c.

The following gauge plugs are used to test the wear of barrels for exchange.

Gauge armourers, plug ·303 inch, ·307 inch, ·308 inch, ·310 inch, and plug lead No. 2.

Plug ·309 inch and plug lead No. 1 are for use with the Maxim gun.

The following tools are supplied for cleaning barrels and clearing obstructions in the bore such as broken pull-throughs, rust, broken cases in chamber, &c.:—

Designation of Tool.	No.	Use of Tool.
Rods, cleaning, ·303 in. :—		
No. 1	1	For Jute, suitable for long or short rifles.
„ 2	1	For use with brass wire, rifle. Can be used for M.L.E. rifles, short, only when fitted with Bush, stop, rod, No. 2.
„ 4	1	For use with brass wire, rifle, short M.L.E.
Bush, stop, rod cleaning, ·303, No. 2.	1	For use with rod No. 2 when used with short rifles.
Muzzle guides :—		
No. 2	1	R.S.M.L.E. For use when using the above rods to prevent "bell-mouthing" of muzzle.
No. 1	1	M.L.E.C.L. rifles. For use when using the above rods to prevent "bell-mouthing" of muzzle.
Plugs, clearing, split, M.L.M. rifle.	1	For removal of split case and bullet envelope from chamber or bore of magazine arms.
Plugs, plain, ·303 in. arms ...	1	Tapped at end to fit on rod No. 2, for use in removal of bullet envelope, and in tamping when removing a broken pull-through, &c.
Tools, clearing, ·303 in. arms :—		
Bits, screw	1	⎫
„ spoon	1	⎬ For removal of broken pull-through, &c.
Bush, bit, screw	1	⎭
Rod, No. 2	1	Screwed at end to take above clearing bits and plugs.
Rods, cleaning, cylinder, pistol, Webley.	1	For use with brass wire.

SHORT RIFLE, MAGAZINE LEE-ENFIELD (MARK III)
Plate I.

SHORT RIFLE, MAGAZINE LEE-ENFIELD (MARK III). Plate II.

SHORT RIFLE, MAGAZINE LEE-ENFIELD (MARK III)

Plate III.

WINDGAUGE.

PLATE IV.

Names of the Parts of Rifle, Short M.L.E., Mark III, referred to in Plates I to III.

1. Blade foresight.
2. Foresight block.
3. Band foresight block.
4. Key   ,,   ,,
5. Crosspin ,,   ,,
5A. Backsight bed.
6.   ,,   ,, crosspin.
6A.   ,,   ,, sight spring screw.
7. Backsight leaf.
8.   ,,   slide.
9.   ,,   slide catch.
10.   ,,   fine adjustment worm wheel.
10A. Wind-gauge.
10B.   ,,   screw.
11. Backsight ramps.
12. Seating for safety catch.
13. Safety catch.
14. Locking bolt stem.
15. Bolt.
16.   ,, head.
17. Striker.
18. Cocking piece.
19. Striker collar with stud.
20. Bolt head tenon.
21. Cocking piece locking recesses.
22. Locking bolt.
23.   ,,   ,,   flat.
24.   ,,   ,,   thumbpiece.
25.   ,,   ,,   aperture sight stem.
26.   ,,   ,,   stop pin recesses.
27.   ,,   ,,   safety catch stem.
28.   ,,   ,,   ,,   ,, arm.
29.   ,,   ,,   screw threads.
30.   ,,   ,,   seating.
31. Bolt cam grooves.
32. Sear.
33.   ,, seating.
34.   ,, spring.
35. Magazine catch.
36. Full bent of cocking piece.
37. Short arm of sear.
38.⎫
39.⎭ Trigger ribs.
40. Trigger.
41. Trigger axis pin.
41A. Magazine case.
41B.   ,,   platform spring.
41C.   ,,   auxiliary   ,,
42. Guard trigger.
43. Stock fore-end.
44. Spring and stud fore-end.
45. Protector backsight.
46. Handguard front and rear.
47. Spring handguard rear.
48. Lower band groove.
49. Lower band.
50. Nosecap.
51. Protector foresight.
52. Sword bar.
53. Boss for ring of sword bayonet crosspiece.
54. Swivel seating.
55.   ,,   piling.
56. Nosecap barrel opening.
57. Inner band.
58.   ,,   ,,   screw.
59.   ,,   ,,   ,,   spring.
60. Butt sling swivel.
61. Sword bayonet, pattern 07.
62. Bridge charger guide.
63. Cut-off.

STRIPPING AND ASSEMBLING.

Rifles, Short, Magazine Lee-Enfield.

Hold the Rifle in the Left Hand.

Remove.	Detail.
Handguard, rear ...	Raise sight, use Tool No. 1 as a lever, and assist to ease off with fingers and thumb of left hand.

Note.—Great care must be used to avoid splitting the guard.

1st Position.

Supported on the left horse underneath the grip and clamped at the band outer clear of the dial sight.

Stripping.

Remove.	Detail.
* Screws, nose-cap, back and front.	Weaker screw removed last.
Nose-cap	With a suitable piece of wood applied against sword-bar tap off towards muzzle.
† Screw, band, outer, and swivel.	
Band, outer, and handguard, front.	Unclamp vice and raise muzzle end.

Assembling.

In reverse order.

Note.—
  † Short side of swivels should be on the same side as the dial sight.
  * Keep the rear end of nose-cap down to ensure screws engaging correctly.

2ND POSITION.

Supported on the right horse just in front of the bed backsight and clamped at the parallel portion of stock butt.

Stripping.

Remove.	Detail.
* Screw, band, inner, and spring	Mark III rifles, unscrew only, remove after fore-end is taken away from barrel.
† Magazine	Release magazine catch.
‡ Screws, guard trigger, front and back	Weaker screw removed last.
Guard, trigger, with trigger	Lift out of seating.
§ Stock, fore-end, with stud and spring	To be lifted level, raising the front end through medium of spring and stud fore-end. If necessary, adopt the method detailed for "removing a tight fore-end."

Note.—For stripping or assembling magazine, *see* p. 17; fore-end, *see* p. 16.

Assembling.

In reverse order.

Note.—

§ Carefully examine fore-end to see that all its fittings are in position. See that the square end on stock bolt is correct and the inner band adjusted before attempting to place fore-end on. If necessary, adopt the method detailed for "replacing a tight fore-end."

‡ Fix the "back screw" first.

† That the stop clip on Nos. 1, 2, and 3 magazines is turned up before attempting to replace.

* Spring, inner, band, should have slight play when the screw is tightened up (test by pressure with large screwdriver).

3RD POSITION.

Supported on the left horse just in front of the bed backsight and clamped at the parallel portion of stock butt.

Stripping.

Remove.	Detail.
* Spring, sear	Place large screwdriver between magazine catch and spring, and turn counter-clockwise.
Screw, sear, with spring retaining breech bolt.	
Sear.	
Pin, catch magazine and catch	Using Drift, catch pin, tap out away from bench.
† Screw, cut-off.	
Cut-off	In the open position, ease out by applying screwdriver between the arm of cut-off and body.
Screws, butt plate and plate.	
Wad, stock bolt ...	Use Tool, removing.
‡ Bolt, stock	The body should be held whilst unscrewing bolt. Immediately the bolt jumps, indicating it is free, stop turning, otherwise the square end of the bolt will damage the threads.
§ Body, with barrel, &c.	If necessary, adopt the method detailed for " removing a tight butt."

Assembling.

Note.— In reverse order.

§ If necessary, adopt the method detailed for " replacing a tight butt."

‡ Hold the body correctly against the stock butt, otherwise the square end of bolt will damage the thread in the socket. The bolt to be left *square* and correct to *gauge*. Do not use undue force or the face of socket will probably be distorted. If necessary, use adjusting washers.

† Screw down flush.

* Engage the long arm with the notch on sear, then place a screwdriver against the nib on the short arm, and press gently down until it engages the notch on the magazine catch.

4TH POSITION.

Sight raised, clamp barrel firmly between bed backsight, and reinforce.

Stripping.

Remove.	Detail.
Screw, spring, sight aperture, and spring. Sight, aperture.	
* Bolt, locking, with safety catch	Remove and unscrew safety catch from locking bolt.
† Bolt, breech ... ... *Note.*—For stripping or assembling Bolt, breech, *see* p. 18.	Raise the bolt lever as far as possible, draw bolt back as far as possible, turn bolt head upwards; the bolt may then be drawn clear. Rifles fitted with sliding charger guides necessitate the guide being drawn to the rear to allow the bolt head to be turned vertical.
Sight	*Only to be removed for special instruction or repair.*
Pin, fixing washer, and washer	Use Drift, pin fixing washer. *Note.*—This pin is tapered.
‡ Pin, axis, sight, back, and sight	Use Drift, magazine, catch pin.
Screw, spring, sight, back	Use Driver, screw, Extractor, axis.
Spring, sight, back ... *Note.*—For stripping or assembling backsight, *see* p. 19 or 20.	Dovetailed in; a special tool required to remove it. *Note.*—The bed backsight and the block band foresight are not to be interfered with.

Assembling.

Note.— In reverse order.

‡ Replaced from left to right, using a pilot pin to give it a lead.
† See that the bolt head is screwed home, that the cocking piece, resisting lug, and extractor are all in the vertical plane. Insert the bolt, pushing it forward until bolt head is clear of resisting shoulder, turn bolt head down, draw back the bolt as far as possible, and press head right down ready to engage rib on body. Force bolt home and turn lever right down.
* Place catch on stem of locking bolt at 9 o'clock. Use no

force whatever, and be careful to prevent the catch from sagging when trying to engage the threads. When screwed home correctly it should be at 10.30.

To Remove a Tight Fore-End.

Turn aperture sight clear. Place drift so that its square end bears evenly on sight seating and grip as illustrated above. Tap lightly and pull upwards at the same time.

To Replace a Tight Fore-end.

Place drift in the trigger guard recess, with its slot clearing the magazine catch and evenly supported on the shoulders. Tapping lightly on drift will cause fore-end to bear correctly on body.

Note.—Fore-ends generally project above the socket, therefore to ascertain if the fore-end is home, look inside the magazine way.

To Remove a Tight Stock Butt.

Grasp the rifle as illustrated. Then tap the butt smartly, about 3 inches from the heel, on the shoulder of the right horse, at the same time pulling outwards with both hands.

The greatest care must be taken to ensure that the stock bolt is free of the body before doing this.

This can be ascertained by inspection, and, if necessary, pressure with a drift inserted from the front of the stock bolt hole in body.

To Assemble a Tight Stock Butt.

Fix the stock correctly into the socket. Hold the rifle with the left hand, muzzle pointing downwards, and place the "anvil" so that it lies evenly on the butt. Drive the butt home by tapping smartly on the anvil.

To Remove the Backsight only.

Remove.	Detail.
Handguard, rear...	Raise sight. Use Tool No. 1 as a lever and assist to ease off with fingers and thumb of left hand.
Band, outer ...	Rifle to be fixed in the 1st Position.
Handguard, front	Rest butt on the floor and slide handguard down clear of nose-cap and remove.
Sight	Use cork clams to prevent damaging fore-end. Fix rifle in the 4th Position and proceed as detailed on p. 13.

Note.—To strip the sight, *see* p. 19 or 20.

STRIPPING AND ASSEMBLING COMPONENTS.
Rifle, Short, Magazine Lee-Enfield.

FORE-END.

Held lightly in the vice.

Stripping.

Remove.	Detail.
Screw, dial sight, pivot	Use Driver, screw, Fork, dial sight.
* Spring.	
Pointer.	
Screw, fixing dial sight	Unscrew three complete turns. Then tap lightly on head of screw to
Dial plate	Loosen dial plate. Complete unscrewing and remove.
Nut and screw protector, backsight	(Marks III and IV rifles only.) Hold screw whilst unscrewing nut.
† Protector, backsight.	

Assembling.

In reverse order.

Note.—

† Bowed wing to be on the right side of fore-end.
* Concave face outwards.
That the following fittings are in position:—

    Plate, keeper, stock bolt.
    Collar, screw, front, trigger guard.
    Washer, nut screw, protector, backsight.
    Washer, screw, fixing dial sight.
    Washer, spring, band, inner.
    Nut, screw, back, nose-cap.
    Stud with spring, fore-end.

MAGAZINES NOS. 1, 2, AND 3.

Stripping.

Right side uppermost.

Remove.	Detail.
Platform with spring ...	Turn the stop clip to front of magazine. Depress rear end of platform and draw the front end clear of magazine behind the front lip. Then ease platform out to the front, twisting it slightly to the right.
Auxiliary spring... ...	Ease off the front of case.

Assembling.

Reverse the motions used in removing. It will be found to assist the rear end of platform into place if it be slightly twisted to the right when being inserted.

MAGAZINE NO. 4.

Stripping.

Remove.	Detail.
Platform with spring ...	Depress the rear end of the platform as far as possible, at the same time holding up the front end; then pull the front end towards the rear end of case until it passes under the front side lips and between the inner forward ribs of the case through which it is sprung. Raise the front end of platform out of the case and tilt the rear end sideways—left side uppermost—and draw forward out of case.
Auxiliary spring	Ease off the front of case.

Assembling.

Reverse the motions used in removing.

Bolt Breech.

Stripping.

(Marks I, I*, II, and II* rifles.)

Remove.	Detail.
Screw, stop, charger, guide.	
* Spring, extractor ...	Use punch end of Tool, removing. Cover with thumb to prevent spring flying out.
Screw, extractor.	
Extractor.	
Screw, keeper, striker.	Use a suitable coin or screwdriver.
† Bolt head, with striker, mainspring, and cocking piece.	See that the stud on cocking piece is in the long cam.

Note.—If it is found that the striker is not unscrewing with the bolt head, draw back the cocking piece clear of cams, and turn till its stud rests on rear end of bolt, then screw home the bolt head, lower the cocking piece until its stud rests in the long cam, and complete the unscrewing of the striker from the cocking piece with the bolt head.

If the striker is tight in the cocking piece, probably the bolt head cannot be moved together with the striker, in which case the striker should be hung up as above whilst the bolt head is removed, afterwards removing the striker with the " Tool, removing."

If undue force is used when attempting to unscrew by means of the bolt head, the striker lug recess and thread on tenon of bolt head are liable to damage.

Assembling.

† Place spring on striker and replace in bolt. Engage bolt head and striker and screw striker partly home.

Place cocking piece in position with stud in long cam and continue screwing. If, when bolt head is screwed home, the shoulder formed on end of striker is not *flush* with the bottom of the recess in the end of cocking piece, withdraw and hang up cocking piece (as explained in stripping), unscrew the bolt head several turns, let the cocking piece go forward again into the long cam, and continue screwing. Replace the keeper screw, being careful that the cut-away portion of the striker is in the correct position.

Note.—It is essential that the bolt head should be correctly screwed home, otherwise the bolt will jam when trying to close the breech.

* To prevent breaking this spring, see that it is properly fitted into its seating before attempting to engage the stud (liable to slip down into the extractor seating).

BACKSIGHT, MARKS III AND IV.

Stripping.

Remove.	Detail.
Screw, catch, slide, b.s., and spring.	Use Driver, screw, Fork, dial sight.
Slide, with catch slide...	Press in catch to disengage worm from rack and draw slide off leaf.
Catch, slide, with worm, f.a., from slide	Using Drift, press catch with worm outwards.
Pin, axis, worm, and worm	(Repair only.) Cylindrical pin.
Pin, fixing head, screw, wind-gauge	Use Drift, pin, fixing head, screw. *Note.*—This pin is tapered.
* Head screw, wind-gauge.	
† Spring, head screw.	
‡ Screw, wind-gauge.	Use Driver, screw, Extractor, axis.
Wind-gauge.	
Spring, wind-gauge.	

Assembling.

In reverse order.

Note.—

‡ A washer screw wind-gauge may be fitted to take up backlash.

† That the square ended projection and not the nib engages in the groove in wind-gauge.

* That it is in correct relation with screw wind-gauge to receive the tapered pin.

BACKSIGHT, MARKS I, I*, II, AND II*.

Stripping.

Remove.	Detail.
* Slide, with catch slide from leaf.	Press studs in and draw slide off leaf.
† Catches, slide, with springs from slide.	Draw outwards.
Screw, keeper, fine adjustment.	
‡ Fine adjustment and springs.	Turn screw, fine adjustment, taking care to cover springs with thumb as fine adjustment is moving off the top of leaf.
Screw, fine adjustment, with spring.	Lift out of seating.
§ Plate, keeper, wind-gauge screw.	Lift out of recess with tool.
‖ Screw, wind-gauge, with spring.	Hold wind-gauge whilst turning.
¶ Wind-gauge.	

Assembling.

In reverse order.

Note.—

¶ Concave face inwards.

‖ Adjust spring and press on head of screw to facilitate replacing.

§ Concave face inwards.

‡ Replace springs with points towards fine adjustment. Fix fine adjustment square on top of leaf, keeping a light pressure against the side of the springs. With screwdriver, compress one of the springs and make it engage under fine adjustment. Taking care to retain this spring, compress the other and make it engage in like manner. Keeping the fine adjustment square, press down and forward, to ensure screw engaging correctly.

† Insert together.

* Make sure that slide (especially slide No. 2) is placed correctly on leaf.

STRIPPING AND ASSEMBLING.

Rifles, Charger Loading, M.L.E., Mark I and I*.

Hold the rifle in the left hand.

Remove.	Detail.
Handguard, rear...	Raise sight. Unclamp and move slide to top of leaf. Apply Tool No. 2 as a lever over the bed backsight.

1st POSITION.

Supported on the left horse underneath the grip, and clamped at the band lower, clear of the dial sight.

Stripping.

Remove.	Detail.
Screw, nose-cap.	
Nose-cap ...	Tap off clear of fore-end, not taken off the barrel.
Screw, band, lower, and swivel.	
Band, lower ...	Unclamp vice; with thumb spring band open to clear pins, and slide clear.

Assembling.

In reverse order.

Note.—Short slide of swivel on the same side as the dial sight.

2ND POSITION.

Supported on the right horse in front of the bed backsight, and clamped at the parallel portion of the stock butt.

Stripping.

Remove.	Detail.
* Magazine	Release magazine catch.
Screws, guard trigger, front and back	Weaker screw removed last.
† Guard trigger, with trigger.	Lift out of seating.
‡ Fore-end	To be lifted off level. If necessary, adopt the method detailed for "Removing a tight fore-end" (p. 14).

Note.—For stripping or assembling magazine, *see* p. 17; dial sight, *see* p. 16.

Assembling.

In reverse order.

Note.—

‡ That the Plate, keeper, stock bolt, Collar, screw, front, trigger guard, and Washer, screw, fixing dial sight, are in position. That the square end on stock bolt is correct before attempting to place fore-end on. If necessary, adopt the method detailed for "Replacing a tight fore-end" (p. 14).

† That the trigger engages correctly with the sear.

* That the stop clip on Nos. 1, 2, and 3 magazines is turned up correctly before attempting to replace.

3rd Position.

Supported on the left horse in front of the bed backsight, and clamped at the parallel portion of the stock butt.

Stripping.

Remove.	Detail.
* Spring, sear	Place large screwdriver between magazine catch and spring, and turn counter-clockwise.
Screw, sear, with spring retaining breech bolt.	
Sear.	
Pin, catch, magazine and catch	Use Drift, catch pin, and tap out away from bench.
† Screw, cut-off.	
Cut-off	In the open position, ease out by applying screwdriver between the arm and body.
Screw, butt plate, and plate.	Turn rifle to remove screw in heel strap.
Wad, stock bolt ...	Use Tool, removing.
‡ Bolt, stock	The body should be held whilst unscrewing bolt. Immediately the bolt jumps, indicating it is free, stop turning, otherwise the square end of bolt will damage the threads.
§ Body, with barrel, &c.	If necessary, adopt the method detailed for " Removing a tight butt " (p. 14).

Assembling.

In reverse order.

Note.—

§ If necessary, adopt the method detailed for "Replacing a tight butt" (p. 15).

‡ Hold the body correctly against the stock butt, otherwise the square end of bolt will damage the thread in the socket. The bolt to be left *square* and correct to *gauge*. Do not use undue force or the face of socket will probably be distorted. If necessary, use adjusting washers.

† Screw down flush.

* Engage the long arm with the notch on sear, then place a screwdriver against the nib on the short arm, and press gently down until it engages the notch on the magazine catch.

4TH POSITION.

Sight raised, clamp firmly at the bed backsight, allowing sufficient clearance to facilitate removal of Pin, axis, backsight.

Stripping.

Remove.	Detail.
Screw, spring, sight aperture, with spring.	
Aperture, sight.	
* Safety catch	Raise to midway position. Use Drift, wire, large, and tap out to the right.
† Screw, keeper, striker	More convenient to remove in this position.
‡ Bolt, breech, with safety pin and spring.	Raise the bolt lever as far as possible, draw bolt back as far as possible, turn bolt head upwards, and draw bolt clear. Carefully remove pin and spring.
Note.—For stripping or assembling bolt breech, *see* p. 25.	
Sight	*Only to be removed for special instruction or repair.*
§ Pin, axis, sight, back, and sight.	Use Drift, sight, axis pin, M.L.M.
Screw, spring, sight, back.	Use Driver, screw, Extractor, axis.
Spring, sight, back ...	Dovetailed in, a special tool required to remove it.

Note.—The bed backsight, block, and protector foresight are not to be interfered with.

Note.—For stripping or assembling backsight, *see* p. 26.

Assembling.

In reverse order.

Note.—
  § Replace from left to right.
  ‡ That the bolt head is screwed home, that the cocking piece, resisting lug, and extractor are all in the vertical plane. Insert the bolt, pushing it forward until bolt head is clear of resisting shoulder, turn bolt head down, draw back the bolt as far as possible, and press head right down ready to engage rib on body. Force bolt home and turn lever right down.
  † Complete the screwing up of screw, keeper, striker.
  * That the spring and pin are in position before attempting to replace.

STRIPPING AND ASSEMBLING COMPONENTS.
Rifles, Charger Loading, M.L.E., Mark I and I*.

BOLT BREECH.

Stripping.

Remove.	Detail.
* Spring, extractor	Use punch end of Tool, removing, cover with thumb to prevent flying out.
Screw, extractor.	
Extractor.	
† Screw, keeper, striker	*Note.*—Easier to take out with the bolt in the rifle.
Bolt head	Unscrew.
‡ Striker, with main spring and cocking piece	Stud of cocking piece in long cam. With Tool, removing, unscrew striker.

Assembling.

Note.—

‡ Replace main spring and striker. Place cocking piece in position and screw the striker home until the shoulder formed on end of striker is flush with the bottom of the keeper screw recess and the cut away part correctly adjusted to receive the head of the keeper screw.

† Screw in sufficiently to retain striker in the correct position. (Screw home after replacing in rifle.)

* To prevent breaking this spring, see that it is properly fitted into its seating before attempting to engage the stud (liable to slip down into the extractor seating).

Mark I* Backsight (fitted with No. 1 Slide).

Stripping.

Remove.	Detail.
Screw, stop	Use Driver, screw, Extractor, axis.
* Slide from leaf... ...	Release clamping nut.
† Nut, clamping, slide ...	Press stud clear and unscrew.
† Stud, clamping, slide ...	Ease out of recess.
Pin fixing head screw, wind-gauge	Use Drift, pin fixing head screw. *Note.*—This pin is tapered.
‡ Head screw, wind-gauge	Draw off.
Screw, wind-gauge ...	Use Driver, screw, Extractor, axis.
Wind-gauge from slide.	
§ Spring, wind-gauge.	
Spring, slide	Spring out of seating.

Note —With No. 2 slides (identified by the head screw being the same size as the clamping nut) the nut, clamping, and stud are not removed until after the spring, wind-gauge, and are replaced accordingly.

Assembling.

In reverse order.

Note.—

§ Convex side up.

‡ That it is in correct relation with screw to receive its tapered pin.

† Insert stud, roughened face inwards.

Screw on. These components are correctly assembled when the nut is screwed until its projection is just past the stud' and is prevented from unscrewing by the stud when the face of the latter is flush with the inner face of slide.

* Press stud, clamping, outwards to give clearance.

ACTION OF MECHANISM—MAGAZINE RIFLES.

Assuming that the rifle has just been fired, there are four distinct motions of the bolt necessary before another round is ready to be fired.

(1) *Raising the Bolt Lever.*—The bolt is revolved, but the cocking piece and bolt head are prevented from turning, the former by the groove in the body, the latter by its hook engaging the rib on the body. Consequently the cam-shaped face between the long and short grooves of the bolt bears against the stud on the cocking piece, and forces the cocking piece to the rear, thus withdrawing the striker from the cartridge and slightly compressing the mainspring from the front. At the same time, owing to the cam face on the bolt lug acting against the face of

the extracting cam recess in the body, the bolt is drawn back with a powerful motion, the extractor moves in and engages with the cartridge and primary extraction of the cartridge is effected. The long rib on the bolt is now opposite the rib-way in the body, and the stud on the cocking piece is in the short groove.

(2) *Drawing back the Bolt.*—The cartridge is extracted and ejected by the action of the shallowing groove and ejector screw on the left side of the body. The bolt is brought up by the projection on the bolt head coming against the resistance shoulder of the body.

(3) *Pushing forward the Bolt.*—The face of the bolt head engages with the top cartridge in the magazine (or with the round placed in by hand) and pushes it into the chamber. The full bent on the cocking piece engages with the sear, and the mainspring is compressed from the rear. The stud between the grooves on the bolt passes on the right of the stud on the cocking piece.

(4) *Turning down the Bolt Lever.*—The bolt lug and the long rib, engaging respectively with the sloping recess in the body and the resistance shoulder, force the bolt forward against the base of the cartridge. The cartridge is now firmly supported, the mainspring is fully compressed, the action is at full cock, and the stud on the cocking piece is opposite the long groove in the bolt.

Pressing the Trigger.

The sear is revolved, at first with a slower and more powerful motion and then with a quicker motion, the bents are disengaged, and the striker flies forward and fires the cartridge.

(The charger loading rifle has only one motion in the pull-off instead of a double motion action.)

Safety Arrangements.

(1) Locking bolt and safety-catch.

To prevent the rifle being fired accidentally (and to prevent loss of bolts on line of march, particularly with M.I.).

(2) Studs on cocking piece and rear end of bolt, and half bent in cocking piece engaging on sear.

To prevent the rifle being fired with the bolt not properly closed.

In this case, either (*a*) the stud on cocking piece coming against sloping face of stud on bolt, automatically closes the bolt; or (*b*) stud on cocking piece strikes full against stud on bolt. If the bolt is then closed, the sear engages in the half-bent, and the action is locked, as the two studs are side by side. The action must be re-cocked by pulling back the cocking piece by hand.

WEIGHING OF SPRINGS.

Method of Weighing.—A spring balance, called a "Tester, trigger, pull" (T.T.P.), is supplied for the purpose of weighing all the springs, upon the correctness of which, in conjunction with cleanliness of the parts, depends the accurate and smooth working of the breech action. If a vice is available it should be used in preference to any other arrangement, as more accurate results are obtained. Once the rifle is fixed in the vice, its position need not be changed, as all the springs can be weighed in that position as described below.

Position in the Vice.—Remove the handguard, rear, so as not to split it with the jaws of the vice.

Secure the rifle immediately in rear of the bed backsight, in a horizontal position, the muzzle pointing towards the left, and the right side up.

Note.—The magazine must always be in position.

Now fully cock the mechanism and proceed as follows.

Pull off.—(The pressure required to release the sear from the full bent of cocking-piece.)

Place the friction roller of the T.T.P. over the finger piece of the trigger, and holding the other end in the right hand, pull in a line diagonally across the small of the butt, steadying the right hand on the back of the left, the finger tips of latter resting on the butt near the heel.

A steady pull should be given, and when the trigger begins to move the weight should be from 3 to 4 lbs.; continue the pull, and when the striker is released the balance should show 5 to 6 lbs. (Rifles short, double pull.)

Charger Loading Rifles.—Pull to move trigger when mainspring is eased $3\frac{1}{2}$ to $4\frac{1}{2}$ lbs., pull off 5 to 7 lbs. (Single pull.)

Note.—The above results are only obtained when the components of the action, including the trigger, are clean and free from oil, or other matter, causing obstruction.* The action should, therefore, be thoroughly cleaned, and slightly oiled; special attention being paid to the following:—(1) That the mainspring is the correct weight. (2) That the bent on the cocking piece and the ribs on the trigger (short rifles) have not been damaged. (3) That there is no packing or foreign substance on the sear seat in the body. (4) That the sear screw is not bent.

If all these points have been attended to and it is still found that the weight is outside the limits laid down, the rifle should be returned to store for special examination.

---

* The action may appear free from oil, but if there is an accumulation of dirty or thick oil in the mainspring chamber, in the bolt hole of the cocking piece, or in striker hole in the bolt head, miss-fires are likely to occur.

Mainspring.—(1) With the striker in the fired position, place the tag of the T.T.P. over the end of the cocking piece, and pull in a direct line with the bolt. When the cocking piece moves the weight should be from 7 to 9 lbs. (2) Cock the action, test again in a similar way, when the weight should be from 14 to 16 lbs.

Spring retaining Bolt Head.—(1) Draw back the bolt until the head is over the spring retaining. (2) Place the claws of tag round the bolt head, and pull with the T.T.P. slightly below the horizontal, and at right angles to the bolt; when the bolt head is released from the spring the weight should be from 10 to 16 lbs. If the weight is outside these limits examine the sear screw and see if it is home and tight.

Extractor Spring.—With the bolt head released, as by the last operation, place the tip of one of the claws of T.T.P. under the hook of the extractor and pull against its spring; when the extractor moves the weight should be from $4\frac{1}{2}$ to $5\frac{1}{2}$ lbs., *if fitted with a spring numbered " 3," 7 to 9 lbs.*

Trap Butt Spring.—Place the tip of the claw under the nib of trap butt; to move the latter the weight should be from 2 to 3 lbs. (converted rifles, and rifles charger loading, $3\frac{1}{2}$ to $4\frac{1}{2}$ lbs.).

Springs do not gain strength; therefore, if too heavy, look for burrs, dirt, or other cause of friction.

MISS-FIRES AND FAILURES.

Assuming that the ammunition is good, these may be placed under the following headings, viz. :—

        A. Miss-fires.
        B. Non-Extraction or Bad Ejection.
        C. Light or Heavy pull-off.
        D. Defective Magazine Supply.

A. Miss-fires.—Probably due to :—(1) Rusty, weak, or broken mainspring. (2) Bent or broken striker. (3) Insufficient protrusion, owing to (*a*) point of striker worn, (*b*) striker screwed too far into cocking piece, (*c*) rust or grit in front of striker, or damaged hole in bolt head, (*d*) wrong pattern keeper screw, viz., a M.L.M. screw in a M.L.E. cocking piece, (*e*) stud on cocking piece or long groove in bolt burred up, (*f*) thick or dirty oil in mainspring chamber, in striker hole in bolt head, or in bolt hole of cocking piece. (4) Bolt not properly closed. (5) Bolt or body badly worn or indented at recoil shoulders.

B. Non-Extraction or Bad Ejection.—Probably due to :—(1) Rusty, dirty, or scored chamber. (2) Broken extractor, weak or broken extractor spring. (3) Hook of extractor worn. (4) Extractor screw hole enlarged or screw worn small. (5) Ejector screw worn. (6) Wrong pattern of extractor spring. (7) Bolt head very loose in bolt.

C. Light Pull-off.—Probably due to:—(1) Light mainspring. (2) Light sear spring. (3) Dirt or packing on the sear seat. (4) Striker not screwed home. (5) Sear too low, or the magazine not in position. (6) Improper form of bent of cocking piece. (7) Screw, guard trigger, front, not properly screwed up.

Heavy Pull-off.—Probably due to:—(1) Main or sear spring too heavy. (2) Sear too high. (3) A bent sear screw. (4) Magazine not pushed home to the correct position, *i.e.*, the bent on the magazine catch not engaging with the bent on the magazine case, and consequently the sear spring unduly compressed. (5) Improper form of bent of cocking piece.

D. Defective Magazine Supply.—Generally due to:—(1) Platform spring weak or broken. (2) Distorted platform. (3) Magazine case dented or rusted. (4) Magazine not engaged by the catch. (5) Damaged cartridges.

Inaccurate Shooting.

As far as the rifle is concerned, this would be due probably to some of the following causes:—

(1) Front or back sight not correctly adjusted or sight slide wrongly assembled (reversed).
(2) Badly rusted or enlarged bore.
(3) Bent, bulged or dented barrel.
(4) Warped fore-end or handguard.
(5) Fore-end or nose-cap incorrectly adjusted.
(6) Wrong bolt.

With regard to (5), the fore-end and nose-cap are carefully adjusted to each rifle, and play of ·002" is allowed between the barrel and nose-cap, and between the barrel and inner band. The nose-cap and fore-end are both given the same number as the rifle.

With regard to (6), the bolt is carefully adjusted to each rifle, and given the same number as the rifle. Bolts must always be used with the particular rifle to which they are numbered for the following reasons:—The shock on discharge is taken up by the longitudinal rib on the bolt, supported by the resistance shoulder, and at the same time by the lug on the underside of the bolt, supported by the rear wall of the cam recess in the body. Therefore if the shock of discharge is not evenly divided between these two supports, the shooting will be erratic; the shot going towards the left if the resistance shoulder takes the greater part of shock and vice versa.

EXAMINATION OF SHORT AND CHARGER LOADING RIFLES.

(Remove handguards, front and rear, *see* p. 15 or 21.)

Number of Rifle.—Should be the same on: Bolt lever, body, barrel, sight leaf, and, in short rifles, fore-end and nose-cap.

Barrel.—Remove bolt, thoroughly clean barrel, and examine. Internally for: Cordwear, bends, bulges, cuts, rust, metallic fouling, excessive scoring, erosion, or other damage. Externally for: Rust and condition of browning.

Nose-cap.—Examine: Boss, for deposit of nickel, burrs, &c.; sword bar, for burrs; screws, front and back, to see that they are tight; screws, swivel, tight, and inserted from left to right.

Spring Stud, Fore-end.—Should be free, and should keep the barrel in contact with the top of the elliptical opening in nose-cap. To test, place the point of a dummy cartridge bullet in the muzzle and rock, when there should be a slight movement, and the muzzle should be returned to the top of the opening by the spring.

Spring Band, Inner.—To be free. Test by pressing with a large screwdriver, against the screw, resting the rifle against something rigid; if correct, a slight movement should be felt. If the screw is not free it is generally due to an excess of wood.

Trigger Guard.—Screws home and fast.

Stock Butt.—Firmly attached to body.

Butt Plate.—Screws tight.

Butt Swivel.—Screw tight.

Furniture.—Examine woodwork generally.

Pull-through.—Weight not damaged, and cord in good condition.

Oil Bottle.—Correct.

Sights.*

Foresight.—Securely fixed, and in good condition.

Backsight.—The bed should be firm, the leaf firm at the joint, it must work smoothly, and the spring must be in good order. See that the slide is assembled correctly on the leaf, that it works smoothly, and that the catches engage truly with the racks. The fine adjustment and wind gauge should fit firmly and move smoothly. See that the ramps are not damaged. With Mark III and converted Mark IV see that the worm teeth are not damaged, and that they engage truly with the rack when the catch is released. Also with these marks see that the protector backsight has the chequered edges towards the breech or its cranked wing on the right to permit extreme right traverse to the wind-gauge.

Dial Sight.—See that the screw fixing and screw pivot are tight, that the pointer is not bent, and that the spring affords it

---
**Note.*—Rifles, charger loading M.L.E., Mark I, are not provided with adjustable fore-sights, sight protector and screw, or wind-gauges on the slide of the back-sight.

the correct stiffness of movement, that the bead is in good condition, and that the plate is of the correct pattern.

Aperture Sight.—See that the screw is tight, that the sight is not bent or damaged, and that the spring holds it in the correct positions.

Carefully wipe barrel and lubricate with composition; examine and replace handguards, outer band, swivel and screw.

Swivel, and band screws, go in from left to right.

Screws must not be loosened to give freedom to a moving part; if this appears to be necessary the fitting is at fault.

Sword Bayonet.—The sword bayonet when properly fitted should have the bolt in the pommel flush with the exterior of the pommel, and the bolt engaging truly with its bearings on the standard, or sword bar of the nose-cap. Should the bolt project beyond the pommel, whether fixed or unfixed, it indicates that grit or dirt has accumulated in the bolt hole, or lodged upon the shoulder bearings for the bolt in the pommel; the sword bayonet would be thereby prevented from being firmly fixed or locked. If the bolt is flush with the pommel when unfixed, and projects when fixed, the end of the pommel is probably bearing on the nose-cap in the case of sword bayonets pattern 1888, and in the case of sword bayonets pattern 1903 and 1907, the rounded end of the sword bar is fouling the socket in the bayonet. This would cause the sword bayonet to be loose, and liable to drop off. This defect should be attended to by an armourer.

Weigh all springs, as detailed on pp. 28, 29.

For testing of barrels for wear, *see* p. 34.

The Action.

Gas Escapes.—Should be clear.

Cartridge Lead.—Examine condition.

Extractor Seating.—Examine condition.

Safety Catch and Locking Bolt.—Should work smoothly and be held in the locked and unlocked positions (showing that the studs on body, recesses in safety catch and spring aperture sight are correct). See that the inner ends of the safety catch and locking bolt are not unduly worn or burred. See that the safety arrangements are in correct working order. To ascertain this proceed as follows:—(1) Turn the safety catch to the rear and see if the bolt is safely locked, turn to the front and fully cock by opening and closing the breech. (2) Try the safety catch in this position; now place the locking bolt in the mid-way position and press the trigger, when the striker should hang up; now push the safety bolt fully to the firing position; this should release the striker, and as the cocking piece moves to the front the sear nose should engage with the half bent.

Note.—If this action takes place correctly it shows that the sear is standing at its proper angle, and also that there is no danger of premature firing owing to worn full bents.

Body.—Examine for burrs, &c., especially in the cocking piece groove, bolt way, and extracting cam recess.

Trigger and Sear.—See that the sear nose engages the half and full bents on the cocking piece correctly, and that it clears the lug on the bolt.

Bolt Breech.—(1) See that it works freely. (2) See that the striker is correctly secured in the cocking piece by its keeper screw. Test the striker point for protrusion and figure (place stud on cocking piece in long cam on bolt and use pattern " C " gauge), protrusion ·04 inch to ·042 inch. See that the striker works easily in the bolt. To do this close the breech and ease the striker, place the thumb of right hand on the knob of lever, and press the trigger with the forefinger; then with the thumb and forefinger of left pull the cocking piece backward and forward. Note if the stud on cocking piece is rubbing against the walls of the long cam. If so, the rifle must be returned to store for adjustment (this defect would probably cause a miss-fire). (3) See that the cocking piece is not too loose on the striker and that its bents are in good condition and not burred, and that the locking recesses are in good order. (4) See that the extractor hook is not broken or unduly worn and that the extractor screw is tight and the head not damaged. (5) That the bolt is not burred or in any way damaged. (6) See that the bolt head is correctly screwed home. (7) See that the bolt closes over the ·064 gauge and that it will not close over the ·074 gauge. (8) Charger guide where present should not be over-loose but work freely.

Feed Mechanism.

Magazine Platform and Catch.—Examine case for dents, &c., noting condition of lips and stop clip. See that the platform rises freely. The magazine catch should stand flush with guide ribs on the trigger guard and its bent should be in good condition. Test by placing the magazine in position.

Feed and Cut-off.—Load the magazine with ten dummy cartridges fed from chargers. Work the action by closing and opening the breech and see that the magazine feeds properly. Open and close the cut-off to see that it works freely and that its projection prevents it from turning clear of slot in body.

Primary Extraction and Ejection.—Test by loading empty cases separately by hand. See that they are ejected properly and that the ejector screw is flush with level of bolt groove.

Note.—Fired cases should be used so that they shall offer the requisite resistance to withdrawal.

TESTING BORE OF BARRELS FOR WEAR.

Before applying the gauges, see that the barrel is thoroughly cleaned and free from metallic fouling, bulges, cuts, or bends. The ·303" plug should then run through the bore. The barrels are sentenced as unserviceable if—(1) ·307" plug runs through, or (2) ·308" plug enters muzzle ·25" (*i.e.*, to line on plug), or (3) ·310" plug enters breech ·25" (*i.e.*, rear end of plug is flush with rear end of barrel), or (4) the No. 2 lead plug enters breech ·5" (*i.e.*, rear end of plug is flush with rear end of barrel).

The measurements at breech end will be taken from the face of barrel.

Note.—In a new or slightly worn barrel the rear end of the ·310" plug does not enter to the line indicating the commencement of the toleration as the front end is checked by the lead at ·3" to the rear of the commencement of the bore which the plug is intended to gauge. The lead is conical, and gradually decreases in diameter to ·303".

Reference gauges are kept at A.O.D. stations to periodically check those used by armourers by comparison with the reference gauges in worn barrels, etc. The reference gauges are stamped " REFERENCE," in addition to the usual marking.

Sentencing Cord-Worn Barrels. (*See* Appendix XXV, R.A.O.S.)

To determine the serviceability of a cord-worn barrel, the following points should be observed:—

(*a*) A barrel will be considered unserviceable through cord wear at breech end when the *fired case* shows clear signs of having *expanded into the cord groove.*

(*b*) If the wear exists at the muzzle, barrels should, if possible, be practically tested for accuracy, as laid down in M.R., 1909 (Reprint 1912). If a 500 yards range is not available, the rifle should be fired at 100 feet range, when the centres of the best 9 out of 10 shots should fall within a circle 1·75 inches in diameter.

Note.—Cord wear in barrels is caused by the pull-through cord rubbing against the breech or muzzle end of the barrel when the pull-through is not drawn through the barrel in line with the bore. The friction ultimately cuts a groove which may lead to burst cases when it occurs at the breech end, and destroys accuracy when it occurs at the muzzle.

Explanation of Various Marks on Rifles.

Mark.	Where Found.	Meaning.
E.Y.	Butt, fore-end, body, barrel and bolt.	May be utilized in case of emergency.
D.P.	Ditto	For drill purposes.
M.T.	Ditto	For use with ·23-inch Morris tube.
A.T.	Ditto	For use with ·22-inch tube and ·22-inch rim-fire cartridge.
	Marks on Barrel.	
Year of manufacture.	Underneath Knox form.	
Rotation number and series letter.	On right of Knox form.	
P.	Left of Knox form	Parallel bore.
∗	Front of Knox form	Rust or cut inside barrel.
∗	On other positions of the barrel.	Corrosion or rust on exterior of barrel near the star.
∗W.	Left side of Knox form, at front end of reinforce for muzzle, and rear end for breech.	Cord-worn. Inspection Department marking.
R.	Knox form	Found rusty by examiner and to be cleaned by armourer.
(∗)	Same as ∗	If marked by A.O.D., to distinguish from Inspection Department marking.
(∗W)	Same as ∗W.	Cord-worn. A.O.D. marking.
H.V.	Barrel, rifles, short, behind backsight; rifles, charger loading, in front of backsight.	Suitable for Mark VII ammunition.

Also various proof and manufacturing marks will be found on the barrel.

Marks on body.

Manufacturer's initials and place of manufacture
Mark of rifle
Year of manufacture
} On right side, close to the stock butt. In converted rifles on the left side.

Rotation number and series letter. } On right side, close to the barrel.

Various proof and inspection marks.

Marks on other components.

Mark.	Where Found.	Meaning.
Rotation number and series letter.	Bolt, fore-end, nose-cap, and sight-leaf.	
S. ...	Fore-end	Early patterns of short rifles. Fitted with spring and stud.
2 ...	Right of butt ...	Early patterns. Plate keeper stock bolt in fore-end.
P. ...	Right of butt ...	Early patterns. Compressed butt.
S. ...	On stock-butt ...	Short butt, 12 inches.
L. ...	On stock-butt ...	Long butt, 13 inches.
L.E.S. 2 ...	On dial plate ...	Suitable for Mark VII ammunition.
2 ...	On slide backsight	Do.
3 ...	On magazine case	Do.
2 ...	On magazine platform	Do.
3 ...	On magazine auxiliary spring	Do.
4 ...	On magazine case	Do.
3 ...	On magazine platform	Do.
2 ...	On platform spring	Do.
4 ...	On magazine auxiliary spring	Do.
C.L.	At right bottom corner of sight-leaf.	Suitable for rifles C.L., M.L.E. Mark I sighted for Mark VII ammunition.
1*, 2	At right bottom corner of sight-leaf.	Suitable for rifles C.L., M.L.E. Mark I* sighted for Mark VII ammunition.
C.L.	On dial plate	Suitable for rifles C.L., M.L.E. Mark I and I* sighted for Mark VII ammunition.

Note.—The No. 4 magazine case and fittings are original manufacture. The No. 3 magazine case and fittings are conversions from Nos. 1 or 2 magazines.

The original slide backsight on Marks I, I*, II, II* R.S.M.L.E. on being adapted for Mark VII ammunition was reversed, altered, and numbered 2. By reversing it, therefore, it again becomes suitable for rifles sighted for Mark VI ammunition.

SWORD BAYONETS.

There are five patterns of sword bayonets in use with magazine arms, viz.:—

    Pattern 1888. Marks I, II, and III. For long rifles.
       „   1903. Mark I. „ short „
       „   1907. „ „ „ „

The various marks of the 1888 pattern differ only in small details.

The 1903 pattern differs from the 1888 pattern in having the ring of the cross-piece and the mortice on the same side. It has a larger nut and stronger bolt.

The 1907 pattern differs from previous patterns in having the blade five inches longer and single edged, with lightening grooves to bring it down to about the same weight as previous patterns. One end of the cross-piece is hooked. (Hook abolished October, 1913.)

The approximate weight of the above sword-bayonets is 16½ ozs.

The scabbards of 1888 and 1903 patterns are interchangeable for patterns 1888 and 1903 sword-bayonets. The 1907 scabbard is special to the 1907 bayonet.

Various Marks on Bayonets.

Mark.	Where found.	Meaning.
*	Pommel	Pommel blemished.
×	Blade	Convex side of blade for future bending.

WEBLEY PISTOL.

Six patterns may be met with in the service, viz. :—Marks I, I*, II, III, IV, V and VI. Some of the latter Marks and the Mark VI are provided with 6-inch barrels for the use of officers and cadets.

The Webley pistol was introduced in August, 1890, to supersede the Enfield pattern. It consists of (i) the barrel, (ii) the body, (iii) the cylinder.

The barrel is connected to the body by a knuckle joint and strap with spring lock. The body is slotted out to form seatings and bearings for the various parts of the breech action, and is provided with vulcanite grips in place of the wooden grips of the Enfield pistols. The cylinder has chambers for six cartridges, and is pivoted on a tubular axis attached to the barrel. The extractor works in this axis, surrounded by a spiral spring, and is actuated by a lever carried in the knuckle joint.

Calibre, ·441 inch.
Weight, 2 lbs. 3 ozs. approx.
Rifling, 7 grooves, 1 turn in 20 calibres, right-handed.
Muzzle velocity, 715 f.s. approx.
Sighted up to 50 yards.

Various Marks on Pistols.

Registered No.—On barrel, body, and cylinder.
Maker and Pattern.—On body and strap.
Date of Issue.—On body.
* On left side of the strap denotes cut or rust in bore.

STRIPPING AND ASSEMBLING.

Webley Pistols, Marks III, IV, V and VI.

Tools required :—Driver, screw, Extractor, axis, Pincers, armourers, and cramps.

Stripping.

Remove.	Detail
Screw, stock.	
Stocks, left and right.	
Screws, guard, trigger, and guard.	
Spring, main	Ease stud out of seating, being careful to prevent the spring flying out. Cock the hammer. Pass the fork of cramp over the spring. Release the hammer. Take hold of cramp and disconnect spring from swivel hammer.
Spring, main, auxiliary.	Lift out of seating.
* Screw, trigger.	
Trigger, with pawl, cylinder catch, and spring	After removing, lift pawl off its pivot. Lift cylinder catch off its pivot, and, if necessary, remove screw spring cylinder catch and spring.
Screw, hammer.	
Hammer, with catch and swivel	After removing hammer, remove screw, swivel hammer, and swivel; also screw, catch hammer, and catch with spring.
Screw, fixing lever ...	Use suitable coin. Release barrel catch, and open the pistol to the fullest extent.
Cylinder, with extractor and spring	Press lever upwards until it causes cam to revolve slightly, and release cylinder, which can then be withdrawn. Unscrew nut extractor, and lift out spring and extractor.
Screw, lever, cam.	
Lever, cam	Lift off its pivot.
Screw, joint axis.	
Pin, joint axis	Tap out towards the left.
Barrel	From body.
Extractor, lever, with auxiliary lever, spring, and pin	Ease out of seating in barrel.
Screws, cam cylinder and cam.	

Stripping—contd.

Remove.	Detail.
Screw, catch, barrel and catch	Press on thumb-piece and slip cramp over spring, thus removing the pressure off the catch.
Spring, catch, barrel ...	Ease off cramp and lift stud on spring out of its seating.
Shield	Special instruction and repair only.

Assembling.

In reverse order.

Note—
* That the cylinder catch projects beyond its recess.

Examination of Webley Pistol.

Note.—
That there are no parts deficient.
That all screws are home and fast.
That all parts fit and work properly, special attention being directed to the following:—

Number of Pistol.—Should be the same on barrel, body, and cylinder.

Barrel.—Bore should be free from cuts, rust, excessive scoring, or other damage.

Cylinder.—Chamber should be free from cuts, rust, &c. With the trigger pressed cylinder should only have but a very slight rotary movement. In the loading position it should revolve freely.

Extractor.—That it is working freely. Extracts and ejects freely.

Ratchet Teeth.—Not damaged nor unduly worn.

Pawl.—That its lifting point is not damaged and the safety stud is in good condition.

Trigger.—That the cylinder stop and trigger nose are not damaged or unduly worn.

* *Cylinder Catch.*—That its bents are in good condition and that it is actuated properly by its spring, also that its recess in the body is correct.

Hammer.—That the hammer catch is not unduly worn and the bents are in good condition.

The Action.—Test to see that the safety arrangements are correct, also that the cartridge is properly fed up and the cap struck central.

Protrusion and Figure of Hammer Nose.—Test with gauge. Should be between ·044 and ·054 inch.

---

* Correct nomenclature is "trigger stop."

Space between Face of Body and Cylinder.—Test with gauge. This ·052 slip gauge should not enter between the body and cylinder at the top.

Weighing of Springs.

(1) *Pull-off.*—Clamp the pistol in a vice by its barrel, and full-cock, apply T.T.P. to trigger. To release hammer a power of 6 to 8 lbs. is required.

(2) *Trigger Action.*—With hammer in fired position the pull on trigger to raise the hammer to full-cock—12 to 15 lbs.

(3) *Mainspring.*—Keeping trigger firmly pressed by finger so that hammer face bears on pistol body, apply the T.T.P. to a loop of twine passed over the head of hammer, and pull in direction of axis of barrel; the weight to move it—$3\frac{3}{4}$ to $4\frac{1}{4}$ lbs.

(4) *Barrel Catch Spring.*—Apply the tags on T.T.P. to the front top of catch and pull horizontally to the rear. The weight should be from 4 to 6 lbs.

Miss-fires with Webley Pistols.

May be caused by the following:—
- (i) Short nose to hammer.
- (ii) Hammer striking cap high, low, to the right, or left.
- (iii) Weak mainspring.
- (iv) Barrel catch not quite home.

Note.—The above may be remedied:—
- (i) By filing away a little of the shoulder of the hammer or replace by spare part.
- (ii) May be caused by backward or forward movement of cylinder on its axis, or excessive rotary movement on the axis due to worn ratchet teeth or lifting point of pawl. Replace defective part.
- (iii) Replace by spare component.
- (iv) Examine spring and catch, see that the axis screw is not over-tight, or replace defective part by spare one.

Pistol, Webley.—Action of Mechanism.

Cocking by Hand.—On pulling the hammer to the rear, the top shoulder of hammer bent bearing on the underside of trigger nose, causes the trigger to revolve, depressing the front end, which carries the cylinder catch,* and raising the rear end, which carries the pawl and cylinder stop. The front end of cylinder catch, coming in contact with the front of the slot in which it works, is stopped and the further movement of the trigger causes

---

* For instructional purposes the term "cylinder catch" is used. The correct nomenclature is "trigger stop."

the spring of the catch which is attached to the trigger to ride up the catch until its front end trips on to the top of the upper bent and jerks the catch upwards into one of the recesses on cylinder, which has meanwhile been brought into position as follows :—

As the trigger is pulled the pawl rises and engaging one of the ratchet teeth on the extractor causes the cylinder to be revolved until it is checked by the cylinder stop. The cartridge is thus brought to the correct position for firing. The cylinder catch comes into operation as explained above and acts as an extra means of holding the cylinder in the correct firing position.

During these movements the front end of auxiliary spring, which is resting on the shoulder of the pawl, is being lifted, and the swivel hammer is being lowered, thus compressing the mainspring.

The above movements are continued until the trigger nose engages in the hammer bent, thus retaining the hammer in the cocked position.

To Fire.—On pulling the trigger its nose is disengaged from the hammer bent, allowing the hammer to fly forward under pressure of the mainspring, striking the cap, thus firing the charge.

Note.—Since the trigger is being held back, the hammer catch is enabled to pass downwards behind the trigger nose.

Rebound Action.—On releasing the trigger it is caused to revolve by the pressure of the mainspring through the medium of the auxiliary acting on the pawl and thus lowering the pawl and cylinder stop, the cylinder meanwhile being held by the cylinder catch, thereby ensuring that the pawl will engage the correct tooth on the head of extractor.

During the movement of the trigger the shoulder of the auxiliary, acting against the rebound arm of the hammer, causes the hammer to revolve slightly to the rear, drawing back the hammer nose clear of the cartridge.

These movements continue until the trigger nose, tripping clear of the hammer catch, comes in contact with the shoulder on top of hammer bent. The spring of the hammer catch being free, forces the catch over the top of the trigger nose.

Trigger Action.—Pulling on the trigger causes it to revolve, thus raising pawl and cylinder stop and lowering cylinder catch. The top of the trigger nose bearing against the hammer catch causes the hammer to revolve to the rear and the mainspring to be compressed.

These movements continue until the cartridge is in position for firing, when the trigger nose, tripping clear of the hammer catch, allows the hammer to fall and fire the cap.

Safety Arrangements.—Owing to the slight working clearance between the various components, any forward pressure on the hammer causes it to revolve slightly to the front, thus lowering the hammer catch. At the same time, owing to the rebound arm of the hammer acting against the shoulder of auxiliary, the front end of auxiliary is lifted and, coming in contact with the safety stud on pawl, lifts the pawl and thereby slightly raises rear end of trigger, bringing the top of its nose into contact with the hammer catch, and thus locking the forward movement of the hammer and preventing it from coming in contact with the cartridge.

Note.—There is a slight movement of the trigger just prior to the pawl being lifted, due to the pressure exerted by the spring of the cylinder catch.

Ejection.—As the pistol is opened the shoulder of the body at the joint engaging bent on extractor lever causes the latter to revolve about its pivot the joint axis pin. The arm of the extractor therefore presses against and raises the " nut extractor " and " extractor " ejecting the empty cases.

As the extractor lever revolves its cam-shaped edge riding against the shoulder of the barrel at the joint causes the extractor lever, which has an elongated pivot hole, to move inwards until just after ejection its bent trips clear of the shoulder on the body and the spring of the nut extractor returns the extractor to its seating and the lever to its normal position.

On closing the pistol, the auxiliary lever acted upon by its spring pushes the extractor lever outwards and its bent is again positioned to engage the shoulder on the body.

Instructions for Cleaning, and Clearing Jammed Pull-through or Flannelette from, Barrels of ·303-inch Rifles by Armourers.

(Instructions for cleaning by the soldier are given in the Musketry Regulations.)

(1) *N.B.*—The oil used must be " oil, G.S." No other lubricant is to be used for the bore of barrels, except that and paraffin mixed when cleaning with brass wire and jute and emery, as detailed below.

(2) *To clean a rusty barrel with the double pull-through.*—All barrels which are slightly rusty inside will be thoroughly cleaned by the armourer. A double pull-through, having a hand loop at one end to enable it to be used with assistance, is supplied for this purpose. It will be used without flannelette (the gauze being expanded as described hereunder) in the following manner:—

Remove the bolt; well oil the gauze of the pull-through, drop the weight through the barrel from the breech, clamp the muzzle guide on the muzzle of the barrel to prevent damage by friction of the cord, and pull the gauze to and fro until the rust is removed; care being taken to draw the pull-through out of the barrel in line with the bore, as any friction of the pull-through cord with the sides of the chamber at the breech causes the chamber to become oval, and thus renders the barrel unserviceable. When the gauze of the pull-through, in consequence of frequent use, ceases to fit the barrel tightly, narrow strips of flannelette or paper may be inserted under each side to increase its diameter.

(3) *To clean rusty barrels with brass wire, emery and jute.*—The eye of the rods Nos. 2 or 4 for wire will be filled with from 50 to 60 strands of brass wire, No. 26 S.W.G., hard, cut in 3-inch lengths, the ends will be pressed back along the length of the rod. The wire, being well oiled with a mixture of two volumes of " oil, G.S.," to one volume of paraffin oil, will be inserted in the muzzle end of the barrel, the arm being held in a vice; the muzzle guide* will then be clamped on the muzzle and the rod worked up and down the bore to remove the rust.

In the case of short rifles the nose cap will have to be removed before using the muzzle guide.

If a barrel is very rusty it will be found easier to remove the rust if the muzzle of the barrel is plugged, and oil poured in from the breech end, and left to soak for a few hours.

After loosening the rust, wipe out the barrel with the rod, cleaning No. 1, for jute, and examine (the jute for this rod will be cut in about 8-inch lengths).

If a barrel is found to require further cleaning, coil the jute round so that it fits the bore tightly, and sprinkle on a little flour emery, replace in the barrel, and after clamping on the muzzle guide work the rod well up and down until the barrel is clean.

The rust being removed, a slightly pitted surface will usually remain; this should be greased with " oil, G.S.".

To preserve the wire when the rods are not in use a cartridge case cut short at the shoulder will be found useful as a cap.

Rods, cleaning, for wire, are supplied in two lengths, No. 2 for long rifles, and No. 4 for short rifles, arranged so that the wire cannot pass beyond the front end of the chamber, owing to the difficulty of withdrawing it if it does so.

Rod, cleaning, No. 2, if fitted with the " Bush, stop, rod, cleaning, No. 2," is suitable for short rifles.

The rod, cleaning, No. 1 for jute is suitable for long or short rifles.

(4) *To clear the barrel when pull-through becomes broken and jammed.*—Screw the "plug clearing plain" on the "rod tool clearing ·303-inch arms," and place it in the barrel at the end nearest the jammed flannelette; compress the flannelette and cord as much as possible, then withdraw the rod and plug, unscrew the plug and screw on the bit spoon, pass this into the barrel and turn, pressing firmly against the jammed material; the spoon bit should be withdrawn after about six turns, and the bit, screw, inserted to withdraw the *cut* material. Very much pressure should not be applied to the bit spoon; neither should

---

* When a muzzle guide becomes worn in the cleaning rod guide hole, particular notice should be taken that there is no friction between the cleaning rod and the bore of the barrel, which is liable to render the barrel unserviceable.

it be turned too many times before withdrawing, as it only chokes when the spoon is filled; care also should be taken that all the material cut by the spoon bit is withdrawn by the bit screw before again using the spoon bit; this should be continued until the bit screw will withdraw the remaining cord and gauze.

NOTE.—No rod of soft metal or wood is ever to be used by armourers in cleaning or clearing the bore of barrels of ·303-inch arms; only the rods issued, which are of hard steel, should be used.

Clearing the Envelope of a Bullet or a Cartridge Case.

Should the envelope of a bullet be left in the lead, or the base of the cartridge case separate circumferentially, the "plug, clearing, split," is used. Insert the plug with the cut-away portion of the rim on the left side of the chamber, close the bolt, and in opening the breech the extractor will draw the plug out of the chamber and the nibs on the split end of the plug, engaging with the envelope or the case, will draw it also out of the chamber.

Should this fail to act in clearing the envelope, the "plug, clearing, plain," attached to the rod and passed down from the muzzle will remove the obstruction.

MAXIM GUNS IN THE SERVICE.

Gun, Maxim, ·45-in.—Martini-Henry Chamber.
Introduced into L.S. January, 1891.

Gun, Maxim, ·303-in.—Magazine Rifle Chamber.
Introduced into L.S. July, 1893.

Gun, Maxim, ·303-in. Converted Mk. I.—February, 1899.
(Converted from ·45-in. Maxim guns.)

Gun, Maxim, ·303-in. Converted Mk. II.—February, 1902.

The ·45-in. gun will only be met with in the Colonies, India and Egypt.

    The average weight for all = 60 lbs.
    The normal rate of fire = 450 rds. per min.
    With Mk. VII ammunition = 500 rds. per min.
    Water in barrel casing boils at 600 rds. with rapid fire.
    ,, ,, ,, evaporates 1½ pints for each 1000 rds. if firing continuous.
    ·45-in. Sighted up to about 2000 yds.
    ·303-in. Converted ,, 2500 ,,
    ·303-in. Guns with Mk. VI ammunition 2900 yds.
    ·303-in. Guns with Mk. VII ammunition 2800 ,,

The conversion of ·45-in. guns to ·303-in. converted Mark I consists in the substitution of ·303-in. barrels, and the altering of various components to suit the smaller calibre barrel. The latter is of the same external diameter as the ·45-in. barrel, and has a special muzzle attachment.

The converted Mark II gun differs from last in being fitted with the Service ·303-in. barrel and attachment for ball firing.

The action, stripping, &c., is identical, for all practical purposes, to that of the Service ·303-in. gun.

MUZZLE ATTACHMENT FOR BALL FIRING.

Provided in order to increase the force of recoil. *Must always be used with Converted Guns.* Should be used with ·303-in. gun when, on account of a badly worn lead, dirt, dried oil, or the water freezing in the barrel casing, the recoil of the barrel is insufficient to work the gun after the usual remedies of adjusting the fuzee spring and oiling the working parts have been tried.

It is screwed into the packing gland seating at the front end of the barrel casing, the screwed end of the attachment acting as a packing gland.

·303-in. MAXIM MACHINE GUN.
Nomenclature of Parts of Gun.

Barrel	With asbestos packing; gunmetal valve.
Barrel casing ...	With ejector tube spring; steam tube with slide valve and keeper screw; packing gland; asbestos packing; two screwed plugs, each with chain, S hooks, and stud; nipple, cork plug with chain and S hooks.
Breech casing...	With buffer spring; check lever with collar and split pin; slides, right and left; trigger bar; fusee spring box.
Condenser, steam	Consisting of Mk. IV G.S. nose bag, with strap; 6 feet of ⅜-in. flexible metallic tubing, with female union.
Cover	With joint pin, collar and fixing pin; cover lock, with piston, spring and stop screw; ammunition label with four rivets; cover springs.
Crank	With crank pin and fixing pin; connecting rod; adjustable with cotter; crank handle and fixing pin; fusee with chain, spring and adjusting screw.
Feed block ...	With slide; top and bottom levers, with spring fixing pin; top and bottom pawls, with axis pin; slide springs; feed block spring; band roller with axis pin, collar and fixing pin.
Lock	Consisting of casing with side levers and screwed head; extractor levers, right and left; extractor with spring and fixing pin; gib with gib spring and cover; extractor stop with keeper and fixing pins; sear with spring and axis pin; trigger with axis and fixing pins; tumbler with axis and fixing pins; firing pin; lock spring, with axis and fixing pins; keeper bracket.
Rear cross-piece	With fixing pin; firing lever, with spring, axis and fixing pins; safety catch and axis pin; piston and spring; shutter with pivot screw; milled heads with leather washers and oil brushes.
Side plates ...	Side plate, right, with side plate spring; side plate, left, with connecting rod spring.
Sight, fore ...	With fixing screw.

Note.—Guns arranged to fire Mark VII ammunition are fitted with a No. 2 feed block and lock, and a graduated plate, Mark III, which is graduated up to 2,800 yards. The solid cams are altered in form. The feed blocks and locks are stamped with the figure "2," the former on the left side and the latter on the side and extractor levers. Guns so arranged are suitable for firing Mark VI ammunition also, it only being necessary to change the graduated plate.

Sight, tangent	Consisting of stem, graduated plate, and two fixing screws; slide with pinion, pawl and fixing pin; tangent sight slide spring; milled head and fixing screw; axis pin; tangent sight spring and piston.

Details Appertaining to Tools and Accessories used for Stripping, &c.

Nomenclature.	Use.

Carried in Wallet.

Plug, clearing	Removing separated cartridge case from chamber.
Punches No. 2...	Driving out large axis and fixing pins, driving small pins flush, and driving home small pins.
„ No. 3...	Driving out pin axis sear.
„ No. 4...	Driving out pins fixing, extractor spring and striker, firing pin. To act as a pilot pin, for pin, axis lock spring.
Balances, spring	Weighing springs and testing resistance offered to recoiling portion.
Pliers, cutting	Wiring axis pins.
Screwdriver, small.	Screw fixing, graduation plate and removing cover, gib spring.
Spanner, shifting	Removing or replacing fusee.
Key, gland and steam tube.	Screwing up or unscrewing packing gland and steam tube.
Pull-through, double.	Removing rust or metallic fouling from barrel.

Carried in Case.

Protector, muzzle	To prevent cord wear at muzzle.
Reflector, mirror M.G.	To facilitate examining interior of barrel.
Funnel, filling...	To facilitate filling barrel casing.

Carried in Box.

Bag, water and nozzle.	
Key, gib, gun-metal valve.	Screwing up or unscrewing valve.
Hammer ...	General service.
Screwdriver, large.	Screws fixing, foresight, milled head, and crank handle. Screws, pivot shutter, keeper steam tube, and stop cover lock.
Tool, belt repairing.	Fixing eyelets and strips in belt.
Plugs, belt Maxim.	Opening out pockets in belt.

NOTE.—The Case, including Wallet, is part of the contents of the Box. It should always accompany the gun when in action, the Box being left in the wagon line.

Carried either in Gun Case or in Case, Spare Barrel and Cleaning Rod.

Rods, cleaning — Cleaning interior of barrel.

With Armourer's Tools.

Mallets, raw hide — For removal or replacement of rear cross-piece and breech casing.

Drifts (copper headed) — Driving large axis, fixing and joint pins flush, driving large pins home, also removing crank handles and ejector tube spring.

FOOTNOTE.—For complete details of :—
 Box, spare parts and tools,
  Maxim, ·303-in. Land (Marks I*, II*, III*, and IV),
 see Paragraph 16738, List of Changes, April, 1914.

STRIPPING ·303-in. MAXIM.

The gun is stripped in the following order :—

Note.—All pins are driven in from R—L, and out *vice versa*.

(1) *Lock and Feed Block:*—Raise cover, turn crank handle on to buffer spring, see that extractor drops, place finger between extractor and stop, raise lock and allow crank handle to come slowly back on to check lever; slide live cartridges out of extractor. Give lock $\frac{1}{8}$ turn to the left and lift off. Lift feed block out.

(2) *Fuzee Spring Box:*—With right hand at the rear and left at front, press box forward until clear of lugs and remove. Disconnect fuzee chain and remove box and spring. Care should be taken to throw no cross strain on the chain.

(3) *Tangent Sight and Cover Lock:*—Place a screwdriver across the breech casing, to bear underneath the gunmetal block and lower the cover. Drive out axis pin of stem and remove with its piston and spring. Close the cover, press in the cover lock with large screwdriver, remove stop screw; the lock with its piston and spring can then be removed.

(4) *Cover:*—Drive out fixing pin of cover joint pin, remove collar and joint pin, and take off cover.

(5) *Rear Cross-piece:*—Drive out tapered fixing pin, grasp with the left hand the left handle of the rear cross-piece, slightly raise the casing and, with mallet, strike top edges of casing alternately until rear cross-piece is clear of the dovetails on the casing. Lift out the trigger bar.

(6) *Slides (R. and L.) and Check Lever:*—Pull out the slides. Drive out fixing pin from check lever collar, remove collar and check lever.

(7) *Recoiling Portion:*—Fold back connecting rod on to crank, turn crank handle vertical and draw out to the rear the recoiling portion. Disconnect side plates by dropping them and springing them outwards. If necessary, by taking out the fixing pin, the crank handle can be driven off with a drift and hammer, and the fuzee unscrewed from left bearing of crank, but as a rule these parts are not required to be stripped.

(8) *Foresight:*—First carefully mark its position then remove fixing screw and foresight.

(9) *Condenser.*—Unscrew union from nipple.

(10) *Steam Tube and Packing Gland.*—Up-end the barrel casing so that it stands on the rear end of the breech casing. Remove the keeper screw and unscrew the steam tube. Unscrew and remove the packing gland and packing.

(11) *Breech and Barrel Casings*† *and Ejector Tube Spring**.—Rest the barrel casing on a table or bench, with the filling hole uppermost, and the breech casing clear of bench; place the left hand

under the breech casing and strike the top edges alternately with a mallet, and the casings will come apart. Lift the ejector tube spring with the point of the screwdriver and tap out the spring with the drift and hammer.

Note.—The breech and barrel casings should only be separated when repairs are necessary. Care must be taken not to strike the barrel casing, and the blows should be struck as close to the dovetailing as possible.

(12) *Lock.*—(1) Release lock spring and lay the lock on bench left side uppermost. Then drive out sear, tumbler, and lock spring axis pins. (2) Remove keeper bracket, lock spring, tumbler, firing pin, extractor levers, and sear. (3) Drive out trigger axis pin, extractor stop keeper pin, remove trigger, extractor stop, and slide extractor from face of lock casing. (4) Push out gib spring cover, take out gib spring and gib. (5) Drive out extractor spring fixing pin, and remove extractor spring.

(13) *Feed Block.*—(1) Drive out spring fixing pin of top and bottom levers, drive out bottom lever and remove top lever and slide. (2) Drive out axis pin of bottom pawls and remove pawls with feed block spring. (3) Drive out fixing pin of band roller axis pin, remove collar, axis pin and band roller. (4) Remove top pawls from slide by pressing them outwards. The springs for pawls if weak or broken are only to be removed by an armourer or qualified artificer.

(14) *Tangent Sight.*—(1) Remove the top fixing screw of graduated plate. (2) Remove fixing screw of the milled head, and lift the latter off the slide. (3) Run the slide off the stem. (4) Remove fixing pin, pawl and pinion from slide. (5) Remove bottom fixing screw of graduated plate and remove latter from the stem. (6) Place the milled head, face upwards, on a bench, then with a drift applied to the rectangular nib on "spring slide" knock the latter down flush with the face, when it can be lifted out with the pliers.

(15) *Rear Cross-piece.*—(1) Drive out axis pin of firing lever, and remove the latter with its spiral spring. (2) Drive out axis pin of safety catch, and lift out the latter, also the piston and spring from their seating. (3) Remove pivot screw and shutter. (4) Unscrew, from the handles, the milled heads with their leather washers, and oil brushes.

Before assembling the gun all parts should be tried in their places separately to see that they work freely.

ASSEMBLING ·303-in. MAXIM GUN.

Reverse all the foregoing operations with the exception that the recoiling portions must be replaced before the packing and gland (10).

Note.—

(14) (2)—Assemble the milled head with the arms of the slide spring outside the lugs on the pawl.

(13) (2)—Pawls and block are stamped F and R respectively to ensure longer pawl being placed at the front.

(11) *—Should be in position and weighed before joining the casings together.

(11) †—Casings should be turned upside down. They are correctly assembled when the bearings for the cross-head joint pin are aligned. When assembled the recoiling portions should be lubricated, worked backwards and forwards to ease the packing, distribute the lubricant, &c.

REPLACEMENT OF DEFECTIVE PARTS OF THE LOCK.

Should any of the components belonging to the lock become defective, they can be replaced from the spare parts, without stripping the lock right down. Proceed as follows:—

(1) *Sear.*—Fully cock, lift the sear, and *hang up* the firing pin with the tumbler and trigger; with the lock on a bench, left side up, drive out the sear axis pin, and remove the sear with its spring.

(2) *Tumbler.*—Fully cock, thus hanging up the firing pin on the sear; drive out the axis pin of tumbler, *pull the trigger slightly*, and lift out tumbler.

Note.—Care should be taken not to allow the screwed head to lift the sear once the tumbler has been removed.

(3) *Trigger, lock spring or extractor levers.*—Release the lock spring, drive out the lock spring axis pin, remove keeper bracket, extractor levers and lock spring; if the trigger is defective drive out the trigger axis pin and remove the trigger.

(4) *Firing Pin.*—Proceed as for (3) but do not remove the trigger. Remove the tumbler axis pin and tumbler, raise the sear, push the screwed head out of its way and the firing pin will drop out.

(5) *Gib, gib spring, or extractor spring.*—This will necessitate the removal of the extractor from the face of lock casing. Release the lock spring, drive out lock spring axis pin, remove keeper bracket, extractor levers, and lock spring, rotate tumbler to withdraw firing pin; next drive out keeper pin of extractor stop, remove latter and slide the extractor off the lock casing; push out gib spring cover, and remove the spring or gib, as the case may be. If extractor spring requires replacing drive out its fixing pin and remove.

Note.—The serviceable components are replaced in the reverse order.

Damaged parts of the lock, no spare part being available.

The gun will fire without the sear, or if the bents of the sear or firing pin are badly worn or broken off, but only single shots, and only by pressing and releasing the double button quickly.

The gun will also fire if the nose of the trigger or bent of the tumbler is badly worn or broken off, but only rapid firing. In this case the gun will fire the instant the crank handle reaches the check lever, although the double button has not been pressed.

If necessary firing can be stopped by throwing the filled end of the belt over the breech casing to the left.

When firing has been stopped as described above, hold the crank handle with the right hand, open the cover, press down the horns of the extractor, draw the lock back and, if there is a live cartridge on the face of the extractor, remove the feed block and belt, close the cover, and allow the lock to fly forward, when the live cartridge, which is on the face of the extractor, will be fired. The lock can then be changed with safety. On no account should the lock be allowed to fly forward until the feed block has been removed and the cover shut.

If, on drawing the lock back, it is found that there is no live cartridge on its face, the lock may be changed at once and the necessity for removing the feed block and the subsequent precautions will not arise.

WEIGHTS OF SPRINGS, &C.

	lbs.	
Lock spring	12 to 14	Lock at full cock.
Gib spring	4 „ 6	When upper nib is pressed down flush.
Extractor spring	4 „ 6	When pressed down flush.
Fuzee spring	5 „ 7	Lock cocked.
Fuzee spring (when muzzle attachment is fitted)	8 „ 10	Lock cocked.
Ejector tube spring	2½ „ 4	To push the case out of the tube. Gun stripped.
Recoiling portion	0 „ 4	Gun level. Lock cocked and fuzee spring disconnected.
Converted Guns—		
Fuzee spring, Mk. I gun	10 „ 12	Lock cocked.
Fuzee spring, Mk. II gun	5 „ 7	Lock cocked.
Recoiling portion	0 „ 7	Gun level. Lock cocked and fuzee spring disconnected.

Note.—The tension of the fuzee spring should always be kept as high as possible consistent with maintaining the normal rate of fire.

EXAMINATION.

The following are the principal points to be observed in the examination of Maxim guns without using gauges :—

Recoiling portion.—See this moves freely. Pull not to exceed 4 lbs. (converted guns 7 lbs.).

Foresight.—See that the barleycorn is in good condition.

Tangent sight.—See that the top edge and V on leaf are in good condition, and that the slide works correctly.

Crank handle.—The crank should bear against the stops. To try this, remove lock and place a piece of thin paper between crank and stop. If the crank fails to nip the paper, the crank handle is probably bent, and bearing on the check lever or against the resistance piece.

Safety catch.—See the spring and catch act automatically when the firing lever is released.

Firing lever.—Test the firing lever by seeing that the trigger bar does not release the trigger before the safety catch is clear, and also see that the trigger is released before the stop on the lever bears against the stop on the rear cross piece.

Ejector tube.—See the spring grips a cartridge case.

Connecting rod, Mark II.—Test whether the correct washer is in, as follows:—Take off the fuzee spring. See that the spring cotter is in its place. Test the length of rod by raising the lock and putting one of the special dummy cartridges, issued to armourers, into the extractor over the firing pin hole; turn the crank handle on to the buffer spring, hold the extractor up against the top stop and let the crank handle come back slowly on to the check lever; if the rod is the correct length the crank handle will require a slight pressure of the hand to force it on to the check lever.

Steam tube.—See that the outer tube moves freely on inner tube when the gun is elevated and depressed.

Barrel.—See to the condition of rifling, lead and coppering.

Lock.—Test the extractor and side levers by bringing the crank handle gently on to the check lever. If the levers are correct, the extractor will be right up. Test the bents of the sear and firing pin. To do this, turn the crank handle on to the buffer spring, raise the safety catch, press the firing lever forward and keep it there. Then bring the crank handle gently down on to the check lever. The extractor should be well up to the top position before the firing pin is released. Examine the face of the extractor for burrs and flaws, at gaps, and firing pin hole. Try the grooves with a dummy cartridge (armourers' dummies must be used for this purpose) to see the gib holds the cartridge horizontally. See that the nose of the trigger and bent of the tumbler are not too much worn. See that the point and bent of the firing pin are in good condition. A broken firing pin can be recognized without stripping the lock by releasing the lock spring with the extractor up. If correct the firing pin will then protrude from the firing pin hole and can be withdrawn by depressing the tail of the tumbler. If broken it will remain protruding.

General.—See that all pins and fixing pins are correct.

ACTION OF THE MECHANISM.

The gun is prepared for rapid fire by hand, as follows :—

1st motion of crank handle.—On revolving the crank handle on to the buffer spring the lock is drawn to the rear, the extractor horns riding along the "solid cams" until they reach the ends of cams, when the extractor drops, partly by its own weight and assisted by the cover springs. The revolving of the crank adds to the *initial tension* of fuzee spring by the chain being wound round the fuzee, and on releasing the crank handle the fuzee spring causes the lock to fly forward, and the extractor, acted upon by the side and extractor levers, rises and seizes the cartridge which has been brought up into position by pulling the belt through the feed block from right to left with the left hand.

2nd motion of crank handle.—On again revolving the crank handle to the front the lock is drawn to the rear, taking with it the live cartridge from belt, the extractor drops, thus bringing the cartridge in line with the chamber, and on the lock going forward the second time this cartridge is placed in the chamber and the extractor rises to engage a second cartridge, which has been drawn into position in feed block as before detailed.

During the passage of lock to the rear the screwed head on side levers (due to the motion of crank) presses down the tail end of tumbler, revolving it on its axis pin, and causing its head, which is engaged with firing pin, to draw back the latter until its bent is engaged by the bent on sear, thus cocking the lock and compressing the lock spring between the firing pin and trigger. On going forward the screwed head and connecting rod tend to straighten themselves, and the former lifts the sear, leaving the firing pin held by the tumbler bent engaging with that of the trigger. The gun is now ready for *rapid fire.*

To fire.—On lifting the safety catch and pressing the firing lever the trigger bar is drawn to the rear ; the bar engaging with the tail of trigger pulls it also to the rear, thus releasing the tumbler and firing pin ; the latter acted upon by the lock spring flies forward, striking the cap of cartridge and firing the gun.

Immediately on firing, the pressure of gas causes the barrel and side plates to recoil for about 1 inch, and the arm on crank handle coming into contact with the resistance piece forces the curved face on crank handle to *roll* on the resistance piece and itself, thus imparting a rotary or downward motion to the crank ; this motion causes the lock to be drawn back and the crank handle to strike the buffer spring. At the same time as this motion is being imparted to the crank the fuzee winds the chain around it, thus further extending the fuzee spring. As the lock moves to the rear it takes the empty case from chamber and live cartridge from belt, the extractor drops, thus bringing empty case in line with ejector tube, and live cartridge in line with chamber where retained by extractor spring and gib. When the

the lock is right back, its flanges are clear of the guides on the side plates, and it is kept in position by the gunmetal block. The recoil of barrel and side plates imparts a lateral motion through the top and bottom levers to the feed block slide, and the pawls on slide engage a cartridge in the belt ready to bring it up into position in feed block. When the energy of recoil is absorbed the fuzee spring asserts itself and, assisted by the buffer spring rebound, carries side plates and barrel back into firing position, feeding up the cartridge, the spring unwinds the chain from fuzee revolving the crank and forcing the lock to its normal position, the extractor places empty case in ejector tube and live round in chamber, then rises and seizes another cartridge in feed block.

At the instant the extractor reaches the firing position the screwed head releases the sear and firing pin, the motions being continued so long as firing lever is kept pressed and trigger bar held back, until the ammunition in belt is expended.

Note.—To fire single shots only, revolve crank handle, pull belt through, and let go handle. This places live cartridge in extractor. Revolve crank a second time, *do not touch belt*, this places live cartridge in line with chamber, and on letting go crank handle the lock places it in chamber; extractor rises, but *does not engage another cartridge in feed block.* On firing, a fresh cartridge is fed up, and it will be only necessary to turn crank handle on to buffer spring to repeat the single shots.

Single shots can also be fired with the gun prepared for rapid fire by pressing the firing lever quickly, groups of four or five shots may also be fired, but this requires considerable practice.

STOPPAGES OR JAMS.

May be classed under two headings:—

I. *Temporary.*—Which are usually due to—
    (a) Failure of some part of the mechanism, which is generally duplicated, and therefore easily replaced, or it may be defective ammunition.
    (b) Want of knowledge of the working parts of the mechanism, or neglect in preparing for action.

II. *Prolonged.*—Due to breakages or defects in the mechanism, which require time and skilled assistance to put right, the gun being put out of action for a considerable period.

The cause of a stoppage or jam in the action of the gun during firing can, as a rule, be quickly detected by noting the position of crank handle, the position taken up by the latter showing the exact place where the lock has been arrested in its backward or forward movement.

Whenever a stoppage occurs, first try to clear, if unsuccessful, see if barrel is home by ascertaining whether there is any space between the front edges of the crank bearings and breech casing, if the barrel is not home it will be due to either the "g.m. valve" working loose or a "fault in feed." The latter can be quickly ascertained, without opening cover, by feeling if the feed block slide is "fast" or "loose"—if the former a fault in feed is indicated, if the latter it is probably the valve that is at fault.

The above has reference to the more common "jams" that occur. There are, however, a number of incidental stoppages that the position of crank handle may or may not indicate; these are enumerated further on.

When a *Temporary* stoppage necessitates the replacement of a lock, feed block, or other spare component, the part removed should be repaired as soon as possible so as to make it again available for use.

If, when the cover is opened to investigate the cause of stoppage, it is seen that the extractor is not quite up, no attempt should be made to raise it. On the contrary, it should be first pushed down before the crank handle is turned over to the front, as by this means all risk of firing a cartridge accidentally is avoided.

Should it ever be necessary to release the lock spring with the lock out of the gun, this should be done with the extractor fully up, and the firing pin hole opposite the firing pin.

Position of Crank Handle.

There are four positions (approximately) which the crank handle occupies when a "jam" occurs:—

1st Position.—At or near the vertical. (Barrel Home.)

This shows that the lock has recoiled the length of a live round, and the "extractor horns" may be above or below the ends of solid cams.

Probable cause.—(1) Heavy fuzee spring. (2) Deteriorated ammunition or worn barrel. (3) Excessive friction due to want of oil, etc. (4) Weak or broken gib spring. (5) Tight pockets in belt.

Note.—With the latter the barrel may not be quite home.

Explanation.—The energy of recoil is expended in trying to *tension* the fuzee spring, the latter being overloaded, or, assuming that the weight of fuzee spring is correct, by a considerable portion of the energy being absorbed by excessive friction between the working parts or excessive resistance due to tight pockets.

FIRST POSITION

BARREL HOME.

Insufficient pressure due to bad ammunition or a worn barrel will also account for a stoppage. When a gib spring breaks the cartridge taken from the feed block by extractor drops in the latter slightly below the mouth of chamber, and therefore cannot enter the latter.

Immediate action.—Turn crank handle on to buffer spring, pull belt to the left front and let go; if stoppage repeated, proceed as follows:—

Remedy.—(1) Lighten fuzee spring, three turns in a contra-clockwise direction. (2) Muzzle attachment. (3) Open cover, turn crank handle on to the buffer spring, raise lock, remove cartridge and rest lock on rear cross-piece. Remove belt from feed block.

"Hang up" the lock by allowing its flanges to ride on top of the guides and the horns of extractor to foul under the rear end of the solid cams. Pull crank handle to the rear and lubricate all bearing surfaces of recoiling parts.

Replace belt, feeding round up to cartridge and bullet stops, force crank handle on to the buffer spring, lower cover, let go the crank handle. (4) Replace lock with spare one from the spare part box. Afterwards replace defective gib or spring. (5) Change belt.

Note.—If frequent stoppages occur in this position, take the ball attachment into use until a favourable opportunity occurs to investigate more fully.

2nd Position.—At or about 45° from the vertical. (BARREL HOME.)

This shows that the lock has recoiled fully, and is unable to go right forward to the firing position, being held back from 1 inch to 2 inches.

Probable cause.—(1) Damaged cartridge. (2) Broken or separated case in chamber. (3) Weak or broken extractor spring. (4) Weak or broken ejector tube spring.

Explanation.—If the distance between the lock and the breech face of barrel is too great, *i.e.*, the connecting rod is not correctly adjusted, the lock does not firmly support the cartridge and the case sets back and separates circumferentially either at the neck or close to the base, thus leaving a portion in the chamber which prevents the insertion of another round.

SECOND POSITION.

BARREL HOME.

Note.—With frequent separations the connecting rod should be looked to, and if necessary adjusted as detailed on page 62.

If the extractor spring breaks the empty case drops below the line of the ejector tube, and thus holds back the lock the length of an empty case, viz., 2¼ inches.

Immediate action.—Strike crank handle a smart, glancing blow towards the rear with heel of right hand, and if obstruction is cleared carry on; if it remains, proceed as follows:—

Remedy.—(1) Open cover, turn crank handle on to buffer spring, see that extractor drops, raise lock with left hand; remove the damaged cartridge, lower lock and cover, pull belt through to left, and let go crank handle.

(2) Open cover, and turn crank handle on to buffer spring; raise lock as before, examine cartridges in extractor, remove broken case (sometimes it will be found that a portion of a case is adhering to a live cartridge in extractor), also live cartridge from extractor and rest the lock on rear cross-piece. Take "clearing plug" with its centre pin fully back, place plug in chamber, lower lock and allow it to go forward until face of extractor is bearing against pin; now press crank handle firmly down, and at the same time with left hand give clearing plug a sharp rocking motion. Now withdraw lock, depress handle of plug, and remove with broken case. Reload.

(3) Change lock with spare one, &c. The empty case will be resting on the projecting nib of spring instead of above it.

(4) Exchange the spring for spare one. It will be necessary to take breech and barrel casing apart. This jam may occur when firing at fairly high targets or big angles of elevation, the defective spring allowing empties to fall back into breech casing.

3rd Position.—At or about 15°—20° from horizontal (BARREL HOME, or nearly home).

THIRD POSITION.

BARREL HOME.
(OR NOT HOME.)

If "barrel home," this shows that the lock is almost home, but the extractor is unable to rise to the firing position.

If "barrel not home," a fault in feed is indicated.

If the feed block slide is jammed, a fault in feed is indicated, irrespective of position of barrel.

Probable cause.—(1) Thick or damaged cartridge rim. (2) Damaged cartridge grooves in extractor. (3) Light fuzee spring. (4) Want of oil, or excessive friction during the final movement of lock. (5) Broken gib. (6) Fault in feed.

Explanation.—If the rim of a cartridge or the grooves in the extractor should be damaged, the extractor in rising will meet with a considerable resistance, and as this is the moment the fuzee spring is at its weakest, the extractor is unable to rise to the firing position and grip the cartridge in feed block.

A light fuzee spring would give a similar result. Excessive friction would absorb the energy necessary to raise the extractor. A broken gib may foul the base of cartridge.

A *badly filled belt* with loose pockets, *damaged strips*, or a *belt box* at an undue angle to the feed block would also absorb a large portion of the necessary energy and cause a stoppage.

Immediate action.—Strike the crank handle on to check lever by a glancing blow with palm of the hand. If this fails slightly raise the crank handle, pull the belt to the left and let go the crank handle, striking it down on to check lever.

Remedy.—(1) Open cover, push extractor down, at same time turn crank handle on to buffer spring and raise lock, remove defective cartridge, which will usually be found in feed block. Lower lock and cover, pull belt, &c., and let go crank handle. (2) Strike crank handle as before, if it fails to go home, replace lock by spare one. If certain that it is not the ammunition (cartridge rims) that is at fault, run the thumb nail along the knife edges of extractor grooves and the position of burrs, &c., can be located. An armourer or artificer should carry out repair. (3) Strike crank handle as before, and if it again jams remove the spring box and increase weight of spring by turning screw in a clockwise direction (6 turns to 1 lb.). (4) Strike handle as before, and if stoppage is repeated open cover, hang up the lock and oil all bearing parts. This is usually the last thing looked for, as the gun should be well lubricated before firing takes place.

Note.—Care should be taken to distinguish between " tight packing " and " want of oil." To discover which fault is present, weigh the recoiling parts to see if within limits—4 lbs.

(5) Change lock. (6) *See* p. 60.

4th Position.—Crank handle right down on check lever (BARREL HOME).

This position shows that a cartridge has failed to fire, or if it has fired, there has been little or no recoil, the lock remaining in a forward or closed position.

FOURTH POSITION

BARREL HOME

Probable cause:—(1) Worn or broken side levers. (2) Worn or broken extractor levers. (3) Defective ammunition. (4) All miss-fires. (5) Broken or flattened point of firing pin. (6) Weak or broken lock spring.

Explanation.—As the causes given are mostly mechanical defects in the mechanism the results briefly explained are as follows :—

(1) and (2).—The extractor will not rise, but the lock will be cocked, and on pressing the firing lever the firing pin will be released, giving an audible indication that the spring and bents are correct.

(3) and (4).—Insufficient or no recoil to work the parts is cleared by turning crank handle on to buffer spring and pulling the belt, if a miss-fire the defective round should be looked for amongst the empties.

(5) and (6) call for no remark; insufficient blow on cap to ignite the composition.

Immediate action.—Turn the crank handle on to the buffer spring, pull the belt to the left front and let go crank handle. If this fails place crank handle on to buffer spring twice.

Remedy.—(1) and (2) Open the cover and it will be seen that extractor has not risen. Only one remedy, replace the lock by spare one, &c.

(3) Immediate action will remedy defect.

(4) Investigate.

(5) If after trying a second cartridge it still fails, open cover, remove cartridges from lock, and see if cap has been struck; if not, or if struck very slightly, examine firing pin to see if it is either broken or flattened. If either of the latter, replace by spare lock, &c.

(6) Try again as for the last, open cover, and if extractor is at its highest it indicates a weak or broken lock spring. Replace lock by spare one, &c.

FAULTS IN FEED.

In nearly all cases the barrel will not be able to go right home, therefore the *crank bearings* will be *showing a space in front*, and *feed block slide* will be *stuck fast*.

Probable cause.—(1) Long cartridge (will not pass on to the cartridge and bullet stops). (2) Damaged cartridge (same as for last). (3) Badly filled belt. (4) Top pawls catching strips after last round has been fed up to ready position.

Jams also occur through the long strips getting bent, or cartridges jarring loose during firing, especially with an old or worn belt. If the belt box is at an undue angle a jam outside feed block will be the result.

Explanation.—The effect of a fault in feed is that the top pawls having engaged behind a cartridge in the belt are unable, owing to some obstruction, to carry the cartridge up to the bullet and cartridge stops in the feed block. The slide which carries these pawls is connected to the barrel, and the result is that the latter is prevented from going home. The distance it is held back will depend on the position of the slide in block, so that the 3rd position of crank handle will not always be the position in which a fault in the feeding action occurs, but is most usual.

Remedy.—The quickest way to clear the above jams would be to remove the feed block and belt complete, and take the spare feed block and fresh belt into use.

The *jammed block and belt* meanwhile *being put right, ready for replacement* when a favourable opportunity occurs.

MISS-FIRES.

Miss-fires are usually caused through some of the following:— (1) Worn point of firing pin. (2) Weak lock spring. (3) Side levers worn. (4) Extractor levers worn. (5) Bent on firing pin or sear worn (or shallow). (6) Defective or deteriorated ammunition.

In addition to the foregoing stoppages a varied number of other causes are given below in detail. They are not of a common occurrence, but have been known to happen, and are included here to enable a detachment to recognize them and apply such remedy as may be advisable.

OTHER STOPPAGES.

A { *At Rapid fire.*—1st Position of crank handle and *Barrel Home.* (1) Broken cover springs. (2) Broken firing pin at tumbler way, or recess for lock spring. (3) Broken head or tail of tumbler.

B { 3rd Position of crank handle with *Barrel Home.* (1) Heavy gib or extractor spring. (2) Strained firing pin or tumbler. (3) Slightly damaged cartridge. (4) Dirty or rusty chamber. (5) Tight packing. (6) Bad feed. (7) Side plates damaged or bent. (8) Buckled extractor spring. (9) Fouling or erosion in ball attachment. (10) Firing pin hole in extractor burred. (11) Screwed head of lock not home. (12)* Gunmetal valve worked loose. (13) Mark II connecting rod too long.

C { 4th Position of crank handle, with *Barrel Home.* (1) Broken feed arm of side plate. (2) Broken stud on feed block slide. (3) Broken top or bottom lever of feed block. (4) Broken trigger bar at knuckle joint. (5) Shutter pivot screw worked loose or unscrewed.

D { AT SINGLE FIRE. 4th Position of crank handle. *Barrel not home.* (1) Heavy fuzee spring. (2) Light charge. (3) Want of oil. (4) Broken head or tail of tumbler. (5) Broken firing pin. (6) Barrel worn.

Stoppage may be caused by cotter working out.

---

* The barrel will not go home.

With regard to the above stoppages, briefly explained:—
"A."—Denotes that the lock has recoiled, at least the full length of a cartridge, but the extractor has not dropped, or if it has, the bullet is not in line with the chamber. "B."—Denotes the inability of the extractor to rise after the lock has gone right forward. "C."—That the breech is properly closed; this can be readily distinguished from a "miss-fire" by the fact that it is possible to load by hand, and in case of 1, 2, and 3 to fire the gun without getting any "feed," and in the case of 4 and 5 not to hear the lock fire when the firing lever is pressed. "D."—The faults given are all liable to be brought about by loading the gun for *single fire*, but if the gun is set for *rapid fire* and *single shots* are fired deliberately by tapping the firing lever these faults would not occur; with 4 and 5 the "tumbler" and "firing pin" are damaged at the moment of firing. It should be noted that it is *single fire*, and the *barrel is not home*.

ADJUSTING CONNECTING ROD, Mk. II.

Five cotters, spring; numbered 0, 1, 2, 3, 4; four washers; numbered 1, 2, 3, 4, No. 1 being the thinnest. When necessary they can be fitted as follows, without stripping the gun:—

Turn the crank handle on to the buffer spring, raise the lock and allow it to rest on the rear cross-piece. Drive down the cotter, raise the lock to an upright position, pull out the cotter with the pliers, and take off the lock with the front part of the connecting rod attached. Now place the washer required over the stud on the boss; then rejoin the connecting rod. Insert the cotter of the same number as the washer used (from the top side), allow the lock to rest on the feed block, and drive the cotter to its place. When a combination of washers is used, the cotter belonging to the thickest washer of the combination should be employed.

CONDEMNATION OF MAXIM ·303-INCH GUN BARRELS.

As far as the *Land Service* is concerned, Maxim machine-gun barrels will, in future, be condemned as unserviceable if they fail to reach the standard of accuracy detailed in Equipment Regulations (see para. 212, E.R., Part I, 1912, Section VI), condemnation by gauging being abolished.

The sentencing of unserviceable barrels D.P. will be done by the Chief Inspector of Small Arms, Enfield Lock, as hitherto.

For *Naval Service* the following is the procedure for condemnation of barrels:—

(1) Barrel cleaned and free from metallic fouling, etc., as with rifles and carbines. The ·303-in. plug should run.
(2) The coppering on exterior at muzzle and breech end not to be chipped or blistered.
(3) The ·307-in. plug enters $\frac{1}{4}$ inch at muzzle.
(4) The ·309-in. ,, ,, 1 inch at breech.
  (*i.e.*, to line engraved on rods, plug.)
(5) The No. 1 lead plug enters the breech $\frac{7}{16}$ inch.

GUN, VICKERS', '303-in.

(Approved November 1912, L. of C., para. 16217.)

Weight (with muzzle attachment)	28½ lbs.
Rate of Fire	500 rds. per min.
Sighted H.V. ammunition	2,900 yards.

In construction, method of loading, and action, it is generally similar to the ·303-in. Maxim gun.

Nomenclature of Parts of Gun.

Barrel	With asbestos packing.
Block, feed	Consisting of: Body; slide; top and bottom levers and split pin; top and bottom pawls (front and rear), springs and axis pins.
Box, fuzee spring	
*Casing, barrel	Consisting of: Casing; steam tube with slide valve and keeper screw; packing gland; asbestos packing; two screwed plugs, each with link, S hook and stud; protector for condenser boss with chain and swivel; cork plug with chain and 2 S hooks.
*Casing, breech	Consisting of: Casing; check lever, keeper pin, piston and spring; sliding shutter with catch, keeper pin, spring and plunger; slide left; slide right, with roller, collar and split fixing pin; front cover catch, keeper pin, plunger, plug and spring.
Cover, front	
Cover, rear	Consisting of; Cover; cover lock, axis pin and spring; trigger bar and spring; cover joint pin with check nut and keeper pin.
Crank	With crank pin and fixing pin.
Fuzee	With chain and fixing pin.
Handle, crank	With fixing pin.
Lock	Consisting of: Casing; side levers, axis bush and split pin; extractor levers, right and left; extractor; gib; gib spring and cover; sear and sear spring: trigger and axis pin; tumbler and axis pin; firing pin; lock spring.
Plate, side, right	With side plate spring.
Plate, side, left	With side plate spring.

---

* These casings are riveted together.

، Rear cross-piece...	Consisting of: Body; T fixing pin; joint pin, check nut and keeper pin; firing lever with pawl and axis pin; trigger bar lever; safety catch, axis pin, spring with piston; milled heads, with oil brushes and leather washers.
Rod, connecting...	With adjusting nut and 6 washers:—3, ·003 in. No. 1; 3, ·005 in. No. 2.
. Sight, fore ...	
Sight, tangent ...	Consisting of: Stem; graduated plate and upper and lower fixing screws; slide; pinion; pawl and fixing pin; slide spring; milled head and fixing screw; axis pin; tangent sight spring and piston.
Spring, fuzee ...	With fittings.
Screw, adjusting, fuzee spring	With vice pin.
Muzzle attachment, for ball firing.	Consisting of: Gland; cup, muzzle, with clamp screw; cone, front; disc; outer casing with split keeper pin, chain, S-hook and stud.

Stripping the Gun.

The gun is stripped in the following order when on the mounting :—

Lock	Clear the extractor by revolving the crank handle twice; raise the rear cover, pull the crank handle on to the roller. See that the extractor drops, place finger between the extractor and stop, and thumb on rear end of the lock, lift lock—at the same time allowing the crank handle to move slowly forward until the lock is released from the side plates—give the lock $\frac{1}{6}$th turn, and lift out.
Block, feed ...	Release front cover catch, raise the cover, and lift out.
Box, fuzee, spring	With the right hand at the rear and the left hand at the front, press the box forward until clear of the lugs, and remove. Disconnect the fuzee chain and remove the box and the spring. Care should be taken to avoid throwing a cross strain on the chain.
Fuzee	Turn the fuzee to the rear until the lugs on the stem are free to be withdrawn.
Muzzle attachment.	Withdraw the split pin, give the outer casing $\frac{1}{6}$th turn and remove it. Unscrew the front cone. Loosen the clamping screw of the muzzle cup and revolve the cup till the clamping screw coincides with the flat on barrel. Remove the cup. Unscrew and remove the gland and packing.

Recoiling portion	Raise the rear cover, unscrew the rear cross-piece T fixing pin, and hinge down the cross-piece; remove slides right and left, and draw out the recoiling portion. Disconnect the side plates from the barrel (removing the left one first). If necessary, by taking out the fixing pin, the crank handle can be driven off with a drift and hammer; but, as a rule, this should not be stripped.
Roller	Remove split fixing pin, collar and roller.
Lever, check	Drive out keeper pin from underside, and take off check lever. To remove piston and spring, turn the piston until its lugs are free to pass along the slots, when the piston will be forced out by the pressure of the spring.
Sight, tangent	Unscrew axis pin and ease out, remove tangent sight, piston and spring.
Lock, cover, rear	Unscrew axis pin and ease out, remove cover lock and spring.
Trigger bar	Remove spring and withdraw trigger bar.
Covers, front and rear	Remove keeper pin and check nut; force out joint pin and take off covers.
Catch, cover, front	To remove spring and plunger: Press the plug forward and give $\frac{1}{4}$ turn by means of a screwdriver, when the plug will be forced out by the spring, and before removing the plunger it must be turned so that the slots are free to pass the lugs in the catch. If necessary, by taking out the keeper pin the catch may be removed.
Rear cross-piece	Remove keeper pin and check nut, force out joint pin and remove rear cross-piece.
Sight, fore	The position of the foresight should be carefully marked; drive the foresight out of the dovetail seating through the right-hand opening in the protector.

Take out the elevating and crosshead joint pin and disconnect the gun.

Steam tube	Up-end the gun so that it stands on the rear end of the breech casing. Remove the keeper screw and unscrew the steam tube.
Shutter, sliding	Press in the catch and force the shutter to the front until it is against the stop, then press in the plunger with a No. 3 punch and further force the shutter until it is clear of the breech casing.

Note.—The steam tube should not be removed if the valve is free.

Assembling the Gun.

Reverse all the foregoing operations with the exception that the recoiling portion must be replaced before the front packing and gland.

Care must be taken when re-assembling the steam tube that the acorn end is inserted into its seating. This is more easily assured by keeping the acorn end in contact with the adjacent channel formed by the corrugations of the barrel casing. The tube should screw home freely when in the correct position.

Stripping Component Parts.

The Lock.

To cock the lock... A convenient method of holding the lock to facilitate cocking, examining, &c., is as follows:—

Rest the bottom of the lock on the fingers of the left hand, hold up the extractor with the forefinger and keep the thumb clear of the trigger.

Place the second finger of the right hand round the neck of the side levers and the thumb on top of the lock clear of the trigger.

Lifting on neck of side levers cocks the lock.

To ease the lock spring — With the left hand support the lock as detailed above.

Press the neck of side levers down to release the sear.

With the side of a screwdriver or similar implement force the trigger to the rear, meanwhile placing the thumb against the top rear end of lock.

Note.—See that the lock is cocked.

Side levers ... Force out the split keeper pin and axis bush, turn side levers to clear extractor levers and remove.

Extractor levers, left and right — Lift off pivot.

Extractor... ... Slide off.

Release the lock spring.

Tumbler and trigger — Press out the axis pins and remove.

Lock spring ... Remove.

Firing pin ...	Raise sear and allow firing pin to slide out.
Sear with spring...	Remove.
Gib and spring ...	Push out the gib spring cover and remove.

Assembling.

In reverse order.

Note.—It will be found more convenient to replace the lock spring last, with the lock in the fired position.

THE FEED BLOCK.

Bottom lever ...	Drive out the split pin and tap out.
Top lever ...	Remove.
Slide with pawls and spring	Take out and remove pawls and spring.
Bottom pawls and spring	Draw out axis pin and remove.

Assembling.

In reverse order.

THE REAR CROSSPIECE.

Firing lever ...	Unscrew axis pin and remove.
Safety catch with spring and piston	Unscrew axis pin and remove.
Trigger bar lever	Lift out.

Assembling.

In reverse order.

Note.—That the pawl engages trigger bar lever.

THE TANGENT SIGHT.

Milled head ...	Remove fixing screw and lift off.
Slide	Remove top fixing screw of graduated plate and run slide off the stem.
Slide spring ...	Remove.
Pawl and pinion...	Press out fixing pin and remove from slide.
Graduated plate...	Unscrew bottom fixing screw and remove.

Assembling.

In reverse order.

WEIGHTS OF SPRINGS, &c.

	lbs.	
Lock spring	12 to 14	Lock at full cock.
Gib spring	4 ,, 6	When pressed down flush.
Fuzee spring	5 ,, 7	Lock removed and check lever held clear of the crank handle.
Fuzee spring (when ball attachment is fitted)	7 ,, 9	Lock removed and check lever held clear of the crank handle.
Recoiling portion	0 ,, 4	Gun level. Lock cocked and fuzee spring disconnected.

Testing and Adjusting Connecting Rod.

Take off fuzee spring. Raise cover and remove lock,

Place one of each of Nos. 1 and 2 washers on the outer face of the adjusting nut on connecting rod.

Replace lock on connecting rod and let down into gun, retaining the lock in the rear position.

The extractor being down, insert through opening in the underside of casing the special armourer's M.G. dummy cartridge in bottom end of extractor over firing pin hole.

Raise extractor, see that the barrel is home, turn crank handle on to the check lever, meanwhile guiding cartridge into chamber.

Push check lever back just clear of crank handle and let crank handle gently down towards rest.

If connecting rod is within limit, a slight check will be felt.

If no pressure is required, it shows that the lock is not fully home (*i.e.* that the connecting rod is not long enough and therefore outside the limit).

If within limit, remove the washers.

If outside the limit, washers must be fitted permanently under the nut which can be removed and re-assembled with the combination tool.

GENERAL INSTRUCTIONS FOR THE MAINTENANCE AND PRESERVATION OF GUNS.

The manner in which machine guns are dealt with as equipment in the Land Service is laid down in Equipment Regulations as under:—

Regular Army, Parts 1 and 2.
Special Reserve, Part I, and Section XVI, Part 2.
Territorial Force, Part 3.

Guns are issued with the bright gunmetal parts painted service colour. It is, however, at the discretion of General Officers Commanding, in the case of armament guns, to vary this colour to suit local requirements.

For cleaning and oiling machine guns and mountings in the hands of troops, the following stores are allowed per annum in peace for one gun and its mounting:—

Flannelette, Mark III	11 yards.
Old linen	3 lbs.
Mineral oil, burning	½ pint.
Russian petroleum for lubricating	8 pints.
Spirits of turpentine	1 pint.
Dubbing	½ lb.
Soap, yellow	4 bars.

When guns are returned to store, packed for transmission, or stowed away in any place where they cannot be readily examined, the barrels and unpainted parts should be coated with "Composition, preserving arms." The mixture is to be made hot, and a piece of flannel dipped in it with which the exterior parts will be dabbed. To coat the inside of the barrels draw a bunch of lamp cotton, well saturated with the mixture, through from both ends; the lamp cotton is to be attached to a piece of twisted copper wire.

In frosty weather, when water is kept in the barrel casing, a blanket or some other thick covering should be kept wrapped round the barrel casing to prevent the water freezing. The working parts of the gun should only be slightly oiled with a lightly-oiled rag. In climates where the temperature is likely to fall much below freezing point, not more than about five pints of water should be put into the barrel casing (20 per cent. of glycerine mixed with the water will prevent it from freezing quickly).

History sheet.—A memorandum of examination or history sheet accompanies each gun when issued. It will be carefully preserved and will be handed over with the gun to which it belongs whenever the gun is transferred from the charge of one officer to that of another, particulars being duly recorded. An immediate record will be made in the sheets of any accident which may happen to the gun, and of the result of each official examination it may undergo. On every occasion on which ball ammunition is fired, the number of rounds fired will be shown, the number of the barrel being inserted in the column of remarks.

Barrels.—A new or part worn, but serviceable, barrel is issued as a part of each gun. This barrel is only to be used for firing ball ammunition.

An old barrel, marked D.P., is also issued, to be used only for drill purposes. A second old barrel, marked D.P.B., is issued, to be used only for firing blank ammunition. On mobilization these three barrels are to be returned to store. In addition, two new barrels (armament, one) are issued with each gun and are to be kept in store and only taken into use on mobilization, one in the gun and one spare. New barrels in store are distinguished by a band of white paint round the centre.

www.ingramcontent.com/pod-product-compliance
Lightning Source LLC
Chambersburg PA
CBHW060215050426
42446CB00013B/3081